IB CHINESE_B_HL

5000 CLASSIFIED VOCABULARY

(By Referring HSK 1-6 (CHINESE PROFICIENCY TEST 1-6) VOCABULARY LIST V2021

Contents

About the Author:

David Yao, the founder of www.LegooMandarin.com and Educational Video Courses Online (www.Edeo.biz), born in china, resides in Kuala Lumpur, Malaysia, holding Master degree from University Malaya, has 25 years' experience in mandarin teaching for foreigners, creating a SYSTEM (more than 200 mandarin courses) designed for foreigners to study Chinese as secondary language. He practices Tai Chi for almost 30 years and establishes Tai Chi Fitness Organization (http://taichifitness.org/) to modernize and promote Tai Chi for fitness and health.

Scan QR code for Lifetime Access to Full Video course together with this book

@ the best price in Udemy:

Our Story

"Share with You What We Know Best" is our Slogan. We start with LEGOO Mandarin and now expand the system into other topics: Bahasa Malaysia, IT eCommerce, Accounting and Finance, Tai Chi Fitness and Qi Gong. You can learn anytime anywhere!

In addition to be a **Contents Provider**, we also provide **Online Systems,** which can be easily integrated with your school or company online system or use separately. We are using Udemy and other more than 10 similar platforms for video courses marketing. The Amazon KDP, Google Books and Apple iBooks are platforms we publishing our textbooks in addition to our own platform. We provide consultancy service to save your time and give you the best tips on how to leverage your efforts using all these amazing platforms. Please contact us for quotations (very reasonable price).

We can assign our trained teachers to conduct **live lesson** through Webinar, Skype and YouTube, Facebook at reasonable price.

Licencing Program to schools & Resellers

We offer Licencing Program to schools! More schools are using our system! You can use quiz, video course, PPT and PDF under our Licencing Program. Customized course development with your own LOGO can be done. Please contact us for details and quotations (very reasonable price).

Licencing Program to Resellers
We offer Licencing Program to Resellers, book stores and other Platforms (Websites, Google stores, Groupons, Facebook stores). We provide contents such PDF books, online Quiz and Video Courses. You can list our contents in your platform. We will share on 50-50 sales basis. We can provide technical assistance to integrate our contents with your system and help response within 24 hours.

Please contact us by whatsapp +60163863716.

David Yao Amazon Kindle Author Central page

For Hardcopy or paperback books at best price with reduced postage, please visit: David Yao Amazon Kindle Author Central page:

http://bit.ly/david-amazon-kdp (USA)

https://www.amazon.co.uk/-/e/B07PR3LTMQ (UK)

https://www.amazon.de/-/e/B07PR3LTMQ (German)

http://www.amazon.fr/-/e/B07PR3LTMQ (France)

https://www.amazon.co.jp/~/e/B07PR3LTMQ (Japan)

https://www.amazon.com/-/e/B07PR3LTMQ (USA)

Preview and download books by David YAO at Apple Book Store:

https://books.apple.com/us/author/david-yao/id584331956

International Baccalaureate (IB) Chinese[1]

IB Diploma Programme

The International Baccalaureate Diploma Programme is a two-year educational programme primarily aimed at 16-to-19-year-olds in 140 countries around the world. The programme provides an internationally accepted qualification for entry into higher education and is recognized by many universities worldwide.[2]

Introduction about IB Chinese and how IB Chinese tutor can help

IB Chinese courses expect students to demonstrate very good abilities of analyzing literature and languages within cultural and social context.

Language A: Studies in Language and Literature

This group of courses mainly focuses on two goals: to improve students' ability of using and analyzing the use language through introducing them basic linguistic and communication knowledge, and to guide students to understand and analyze various literature works through discussing writing techniques, context and etc. They are expected to demonstrate good skills in appreciating literary works and writing long essays. Ability of examining a fiction or cultural phenomenon within certain historical and cultural background is also crucial.

---

[1] https://www.hkexcel.org/post/introduction-about-ib-chinese-and-how-ib-chinese-tutor-can-help

https://www.ibo.org/programmes/diploma-programme/curriculum

[2] (Wikipedia)

. Students could choose two languages from this group to get a bilingual diploma. For example, they could take both Chinese A Language Literature and English A Language and Literature. This subject provides two courses: Language A: Literature and Language A: Language and Literature.

The Comparation of HSK with Oversea Main Chinese Tests

China Standard (Similar with K1-K12)	New HSK (after Year 2009)	Accumulated (or Total) Vocabulary	Chinese Language Proficiency Scales for Speakers of Other Languages (CLPS)	International Baccalaureate (IB)						
				Group 1 - Studies in language and literature				Group 2 - Language acquisition		
				Chinese_A_Language_and_literature_HL	Chinese_A_Language_and_literature_SL	Chinese_A_Literature_HL	Chinese_A_Literature_SL	Chinese_B_HL	Chinese_B_SL	Mandarin_ab_initio
Year (10-12)	(HSK 11) Advanced (Old HSK before 2009)	> 8,000		YES	YES	YES	YES	YES		
Year (7-9)	HSK 6	> 5,000	Level V	YES	YES	YES	YES	YES	YES	
Year (5-6)	HSK 5	2500	Level V	YES	YES	YES	YES	YES	YES	YES
Year (3-4)	HSK 4	1200	Level IV	YES	YES	YES	YES	YES	YES	YES
Year (2-3)	HSK 3	600	Level III	YES	YES	YES	YES	YES	YES	YES
Year (1-2)	HSK 2	300	Level II	YES	YES	YES	YES	YES	YES	YES
Year (1-2)	HSK 1	150	Level I	YES	YES	YES	YES	YES	YES	YES

Language A: Literature

This course focuses on literature studies for students whose mother tongue is Chinese. This course is divided into four parts, and each part introduces a certain group of literary works. After studying this course, students will have a very clear view of literary works from various historical backgrounds, cultures and genres. Students are expected to analyze literary works using various perspectives, particularly analyzing the social and cultural context. They will not only learn how to conduct textual analysis but also learn how to write long comparative essays on more than texts.

This course enables teachers to pick up literary works from a prescribed list. There are four parts: works in translation, detailed study, literary genres, and options in which works are freely chosen.

This course is available in both Standard Level and Higher Level. Higher Level requires students to spend 240 class hours as the minimum, and Standard Level students need to spend 150 class hours. Higher Level students should study 13 literary works and Standard Level students need 10. Besides, the assessment of Higher Level is much more difficult than the Standard Level. In paper 1 Literary Analysis, all students will analyze one unseen article but Standard Level students will have two guiding questions. In Individual Oral Commentary, Standard Level students will do a 10-minutes commentary on one work from part 2, but Higher Level students are required to talk about poetry in part 2 within the 10 minutes, followed by a discussion on one of the other 2 part works. In paper 2, students will have the same essay questions but as Higher Level students study more literary works have more time to finish their writing, they often choose to take three or more texts into analysis rather than 2 works.

Language A: Language and Literature

This course is divided into four parts, two focusing on language and two on literature. Students are guided to think about the meaning of language we use everyday and to explore how the use of language has influenced our life, while they also need to study literary works to improve their skills of appreciating literature and to demonstrate their ability of understanding cultural and social context. Students will not only study fictions but also non-literature works, such as advertisement, news report and historical documentaries.

This course is available in both Standard Level and Higher Level. Higher Level requires students to spend 240 class hours as the minimum, and Standard Level students need to spend 150 class hours. Higher Level students should study 6 literary works and Standard Level students need 4.

The first part is language in cultural context, and text will be chosen from a wide range of medias and forms. The second part is language and mass communication. The third part is literature – texts and contexts. Both Higher Level and Standard Level students will study one work translated from another language and one work written in Chinese. But Higher Level students are required to study one more literary work, which can be freely chosen. The fourth part is literature – critical study; texts will be chosen from a prescribed list.

The assessment of Higher Level and Standard Level are similar, even though Higher Level students have more time in the test to write longer essays. 70% of the assessment will be external, including paper 1 writing in textual analysis, paper 2 essay writing to use literary works to respond to certain questions, and a written task. The rest 30% internal assessment will be individual oral commentary and further oral commentary. What should be noted is that, while Standard Level students only need to analyze one article, Higher Level students need to conduct comparative analysis of two unseen articles.

Language Acquisition

Students are required to take at least one subject from this group. Students who study Chinese as the second language can take one course in this group. It does not require understanding of literature works but focuses on the ability of understanding and using Chinese in various situations in daily life, such as writing emails, diaries and public speeches. There are two subjects available in Chinese in this group: Chinese ab initio and Chinese B.

Chinese ab initio

This course is for beginners, for example, students whose first language is English but have a little experience in learning Chinese or have no experience. It is only available in Standard Level.

In this class, students will learn how to use Chinese to express their ideas in daily conversations, to understand some reading tasks and to use Chinese to write very simple and short paragraphs. After finishing this course, students are expected to demonstrate good writing and speaking skills in discussing everyday topics, such as self introduction, weather, travelling, shopping, family members and so on. This course may sound difficult for foreign students who have very limited exposure to Chinese, for example, they don't have chances to speak Chinese out of class. But no worries, as long as they are interested in Chinese and they are willing to spend time in practicing, they will make great progresses.

Chinese B

If students have some experience of learning Chinese, they could choose Chinese B. Chinese B courses are available in both Higher Level and Standard Level. Chinese B courses focuses on various topics: communication and media, global issues, social relationships, and optional topics including cultural diversity, customs and traditions, health, leisure, science and technology for students to pick up 2. Through reading articles and writing on those topics, students will enlarge their vocabularies and improve their abilities of writing well-structured sentences and well-organized essays. They will be guided to write blogs, diaries, emails and letters, public speeches and debating speeches to improve their skills of organizing an argument and expressing their ideas.

Students will be assessed from three aspects. The first is reading skills. They will read several short articles in their paper 1 test, to answer following questions so that teachers can examine if students could understand very detailed information and difficult vocabularies. The second part is writing test in paper 2. Students will choose one question from a list and to write a short essay in different formats. They need to be familiar with various formats and to be able to talk about various topics. So it is important to remember relevant sentences and examples in their daily studies when they read textbooks or extra reading exercise. They also need to organise their writing in a very clear and logical way. Besides, they will finish their written assignment, which will test their ability of reading, summarising and writing. The third part is speaking and listening skills. All Chinese B students will do oral test, both individual oral speaking and presentation with friends. Good pronunciation and fluent expression is crucial. In the new syllabus, they will have a listening test that they need to answer questions based on what they have listened, which requires them to develop quick understanding of Chinese.

Tips on Studying Chinese

At the first sight IB Chinese courses may look complicated, but there are always very useful ways to succeed. Here are tips shared by IB tutors.

Firstly, practice makes perfect. Students should spend more time to read and write in Chinese no matter they take Chinese A or B. Students may find they don't have the opportunities to practice Chinese and usually they don't have homework. What they need is to find reading and writing materials on their own or ask an IB tutor for help. It is through practice day by day that we can develop good vocabularies and good knowledge of Chinese culture.

Secondly, revise. Always rethink about your homework or papers after your teacher graded it. Read comment carefully and ask questions when you are not sure about what it means. Revise everything. This can help you to polish your writing and in the next time when you write a similar topic or analyzing a similar example, you will know avoid the same mistakes.

Thirdly, find a sample to imitate. Learning a language is always about imitation. We imitate other people how to talk, how to use certain expressions and how to write a well-organized essay. Students often say: "I know this is a good quotation, but how to elaborate it? I don't know what to do after I put it here." How to solve that problem? Find a sample, or find someone who can write that sample for you and teach you how to analyze a quotation or a secondary source. Students meet this problem not only when they write their paper 2 but also in their extended essay if they choose to do Chinese. It is very normal that they have no idea what a 4800-characters should look like; even university students will write such a long paper only in their third or final years. This is what IB tutor can help. They have experienced in writing research papers on various topics so that they can help you with structuring your argument and conducting academic research. Always take Chinese as a language, not just a subject; then you will find the beauty of the Chinese literature and culture. IB Chinese tutor will always be a very good choice if you need someone to listen to your worries, to help you to find out your weakness and to help you to improve.

Language B (SL and HL)

The language B Standard Level (SL) and language B Higher Level (HL) courses are language acquisition courses for students with some previous experience of the target language.

The distinction between language B SL and HL can been seen in the number of recommended teaching hours, the level of competency the student is expected to develop in receptive, productive and interactive skills, and that HL students are required to study two literary works originally written in the target language.

Students develop the ability to communicate in the target language through the study of language, themes and texts. In doing so, they also develop conceptual understandings of how language works. Communication is evidenced through receptive, productive and interactive skills across a range of contexts and purposes that are appropriate to the level of the course (and beyond those for language ab initio).

The language B syllabus is organized into five prescribed themes: identities, experiences, human ingenuity, social organization and sharing the planet. Optional recommended topics and possible questions for each theme are presented in the guide, but are not prescribed.

Key features of the curriculum and assessment models

Available at standard (SL) and higher level (HL)

The recommended teaching time to complete the course is 150 hours for SL and 240 hours for HL

Knowledge of vocabulary and grammar (the what of language) is reinforced and extended by understanding audience, context, purpose, meaning and variation (the why and how of language)

The development of international-mindedness is one of the key aims of the course

The prescribed themes of the course are inspired by the transdisciplinary themes of the Primary Years Programme (PYP) and the global contexts of the Middle Years Programme (MYP)

Students are exposed to a variety of authentic text types in relation to the prescribed themes and related course content

Students describe situations, narrate events, make comparisons, explain problems, and state and support their personal opinions on a variety of topics relating to course content

Students produce a wide variety of oral and written texts for audiences, contexts and purposes associated with academic and personal interests

At HL, students are required to study two literary works originally written in the target language, and are expected to extend the range and complexity of the language they use and understand in order to communicate

Students are assessed both externally and internally

External assessment consists of Paper 1: productive skills—writing (a written response to a task) and Paper 2: receptive skills—with separate sections for listening (demonstrating understanding of three audio passages) and reading (demonstrating understanding of three written passages)

Internal assessment at SL consists of an individual oral assessment—productive and interactive skills (a presentation by the student and a follow-up discussion based on a visual stimulus linked to one of the prescribed themes of the course, and a general conversation with the teacher based on at least one additional theme of the course)

Internal assessment at HL consists of an individual oral assessment—productive and interactive skills (a presentation by the student and a follow-up discussion based on an extract from one of the literary works studied during the course, and a general conversation with the teacher using one or more of the five prescribed themes of the course as a starting point)

Preface IB Chinese_B_HL 5000 Classified Vocabulary V2021

By referring to Cambridge IGCSE Chinese, Edexcel IGCSE Chinese (another two examination board) and HSK (Chicness Proficiency Test), IB Chinese Syllabus, AP Chinese, SAT Chinese, Online Chinese Courses, BCT (Business Chinese), combining our 25 years' experience in Teaching and editing our own materials, here is the "LIFE SAVING" book called by many students for their exams. The book give a quick revision for your coming exam! Thanks for your support for us creating better contents for you! It takes our years' painful effort to edit. Grab it!

By Referring HSK 1-6 (Chinese Proficiency Test 1-6) Vocabulary List and There are total 150 vocabularies with the possible Best English Translation for your better understanding with our many years' experience in HSK and GCSE teaching. We also give HSK level classifications which will give you a cross reference for your Chinese standard. The vocabularies are classified into following 12 categories then ranked according HSK levels.

1 名词   míngcí   Noun

2 动词   dòngcí   Verb

3 形容词   xíngróngcí   Adjective

4 代词   dàicí   Pronouns

5 数词   shù cí   Numeral

6 量词   liàngcí   Classifier; Measure Word (MW)

7 副词   fùcí   Adverb

8 连词   liáncí   Conjunction

9 介词   jiècí   Preposition

10 助词   zhùcí   Particle

11 叹词   tàn cí   Interjection

12 象声词 xiàngshēngcí onomatopoeia

Many students call it "LIFE SAVING" for their exam. The book give a quick revision for your coming exam! Grab it! Thanks for your support for us creating better contents for you! It takes our years' painful effort to edit and please respect our copy rights.

This is the vocabulary list for New HSK 9! Is there any HSK 9? Yes, the initial Classification from 1992 to 2009. There are total 8000 vocabularies. New HSK (after 2009) which cut the vocabulary to 5000, just want to set a lower passing bar for students who take Chinese as second language or foreign language. There are around 100,000 vocabularies in comprehensive Chinese dictionary. The new HSK 5000 vocabularies only account for 5%, which is far from enough for students to continue their college in China taught in Chinese. For advance level oversea Chinese examinations like IB Chinese_A_Language_and_literature_HL, IB Chinese_A_Literature_HL, IB Chinese_B_HL, SAT Chinese, AP Chinese, Edexcel A LEVEL Chinese 9CN0-01,02,03 (OLD 6CN0), Edexcel AS Chinese 8CN0-01,02,03 (OLD 6CN0), CIE IGCSE First Language (0509), CIE IGCSE Second Language (0523), the vocabulary involved are far more than HSK 5000 vocabularies.

Due to this, we continue to update our HSK 9 Vocabularies with the possible Best English Translation for your better understanding with our many years' experience in HSK and GCSE teaching since 2009! By referring oversea Chinese examinations and China Education Ministry official vocabulary list up to high school, similar to K12 in USA, we choose the full vocabulary list specified by Education Minstry of P.R.China as an addition to our HSK 6 Vocabularies.

The full list summary and comparing with HSK (New after 2009).

甲级词(1033); (HSK 1-4)

乙级词(2018); (HSK 5-6)

丙级词(2202) ; (HSK 6)

丁级词(3569) (HSK 9 before 2009)

We also add more sentences to illustrate how to apply certain vocabularies in context. All sentences are chosen from authority resources such as Oxford dictionary, Cambridge dictionary etc.

Many students call it "LIFE SAVING" for their exam. The book give a quick revision for your coming exam! Grab it! Thanks for your support for us creating better contents for you! It takes our years' painful effort to edit and please respect our copy rights.

How to use this book effectively?

Tips:

Tally the words you DON'T know in front

1. Tally the words you DON'T know in front. This will shorten your Vocabulary. If you tally a work 4 times. This means this word bullies you FOUR times. Then? Remember or Kill it!

Why many students call it "LIFE SAVING" for their exam.

2 For students who taking IGCSE Chinese, IB, or HSK, the HSK Classifications will give you cross reference. If your level are IB HL (HSK 6), all HSK 6 words you need to know the meaning and reading, HSK 5 and lower words you should know how to write out. If your level are IGCSE (HSK 4), all HSK 4 words you need to know the meaning and reading, HSK 4 and lower words you should know how to write out. This will help you to highlight the priorities of your study. That's why many students call it "LIFE SAVING" for their exam.

The new HSK (Chinese Proficiency Test) Introduction:

The new HSK (Chinese Proficiency Test) is an international standardized exam that tests and rates Chinese language proficiency. It assesses non-native Chinese speakers' abilities in using the Chinese language in their daily, academic and professional lives. HSK consists of six levels, namely the HSK (level I), HSK (level II), HSK (level III), HSK (level IV), HSK (level V), and HSK (level VI).

II. Test Levels

New HSK	Vocabulary
HSK (Level I)	150
HSK (Level II)	300
HSK (Level III)	600
HSK (Level IV)	1200
HSK (Level V)	2500
HSK (Level VI)	Over 5,000

1. Test takers who are able to pass the HSK (Level I) can understand and use very simple Chinese words and phrases, meet basic needs for communication and possess the ability to further their Chinese language studies.

2. Test takers who are able to pass the HSK (Level II) have an excellent grasp of basic Chinese and can communicate in simple and routine tasks requiring a simple and direct exchange of information on familiar and routine matters.

3. Test takers who are able to pass the HSK (Level III) can communicate in Chinese at a basic level in their daily, academic and professional lives. They can manage most communication in Chinese when travelling in China.

4. Test takers who are able to pass the HSK (Level IV) can converse in Chinese on a wide range of topics and are able to communicate fluently with native Chinese speakers.

5. Test takers who are able to pass the HSK (Level V) can read Chinese newspapers and magazines, enjoy Chinese films and plays, and give a full-length speech in Chinese.

6. Test takers who are able to pass the HSK (Level VI) can easily comprehend written and spoken information in Chinese and can effectively express themselves in Chinese, both orally and on paper.

The levels of the new HSK correspond to the levels of the Chinese Language Proficiency Scales for Speakers of Other Languages (CLPS) and the Common European Framework of Reference for Languages (CEF), GCSE, IGCSE, AS, A Level (A1, A2), IB, SAT, AP as follows:

New HSK	Vocabulary	CLPS	CEF	GCSE/IGCSE	AS, A Level (A1, A2)	IB (SL)	IB (HL)	SAT	AP
HSK (Level VI)	Over 5,000	Level V	C2				5000		
HSK (Level V)	2500		C1		2500	2500	2500	2500	2500
HSK (Level IV)	1200	Level IV	B2	1200	1200	1200	1200	1200	1200
HSK (Level III)	600	Level III	B1	600	600	600	600	600	600
HSK (Level II)	300	Level II	A2	300	300	300	300	300	300
HSK (Level I)	150	Level I	A1	150	150	150	150	150	150

The HSK (Level V) assesses test takers' abilities in the application of everyday Chinese. It is the counterpart of the Level V of the Chinese

Language Proficiency Scales for Speakers of Other Languages and the C1 Level of the Common European Framework of Reference (CEF). Test takers who are able to pass the HSK (Level V) can read Chinese newspapers and magazines, enjoy Chinese films and plays and give a full-length speech in Chinese.

I. Test Target

The HSK (Level V) is intended for students who have studied Chinese 2-4 class hours per week for more than two academic years. These students have mastered 2,500 commonly used words and related grammar patterns.

II. Test Content

The HSK (Level V) test is made up of listening comprehension, reading comprehension and writing sections and contains a total of 100 items.

Section		Number of Items		Duration (Min)
I. Listening	Part I	20	45	About 30
	Part II	25		
Filling out the answer sheet(Mark your answers for listening comprehension on Answer Sheet)				5
II. Reading	Part I	15	45	45
	Part II	10		
	Part III	20		
III. Writing	Part I	8	10	40
	Part II	2		
Total	/		100	About 120

The test will last for 125 minutes in total (including 5 minutes in which the test takers fill in personal information).

David YAO, Founder of

https://edeo.biz/shop   &   www.legoomandarin.com

21 March 2019

What's new in Version 2021?

Add similar words to compare the meaning or usage:

Verb + Object (Things, Sth.)

喝水 h ē shu ǐ   Drink water

把 + Object (Things) + Verb (Have Sth. done)

把水喝了   b ǎ shu ǐ h ē le   Drink water

打开书   d ǎ k ā i sh ū   Open the book

把书打开   b ǎ sh ū d ǎ k ā i Open the book

吃饭　　　　chī fàn　　　　　　　　Eat meal (eat food)

把饭吃了。　bǎ fàn chī le.　　　　　Have the meal eaten.

吃完饭　　　Chī wán fàn　　　　　　Finish meal

把 + Object (Things) + Verb + Complementary (which shows the result of action)

把饭吃完　　bǎ fàn chī wán　　　Have the meal finished (Finish the meal!)

把饭吃干净　　　bǎ fàn chī gān jìng　　　　　Eat all cleanly.

Compare with another Passive words 被 (by)

Object (Things, Sth.) + 被 + （Sb.） + Verb　(Sth. Done by Sb.)

饭被他吃了。　　fàn bèi tā chī le.　　　　　The meal was eaten by him.

饭被他吃完了。　Fàn bèi tā chī wán liǎo. The meal was eaten all by him.

饭被他吃干净。　Fàn bèi tā chī gān jìng. The meal was eaten cleanly by him.

Add similar words to compare the meaning or usage:

…点钟　　…diǎn zhōng　(名)... O'clock

一点钟　　Yī diǎn zhōng (名) one o'Clock　HSK 1　new

两点钟　　Liǎng diǎn zhōng　(名) two o'clock　HSK 1　new

Comparing with 小时

小时　xiǎoshí　(名) hour HSK 2　new

半小时　　bàn xiǎoshí　half an hour.

两个小时　liǎng gè xiǎoshí　two hours

一天有 24 个小时。　yī tiān yǒu Èrshísì gè xiǎoshí.　There are twenty-four hours in a day

Fine difference highlighted!

得　　dé　　(动) get; gain; obtain:　HSK 4　new

得到　dédào　　(动) get; obtain; gain; receive

得　　děi　(动) must; have to:

More illustrations:

顿　dùn (量) （used for number of times of scold, meal, persuade)　HSK 4　new

三顿饭	sān dùn fàn	three meals.
挨了一顿骂	āi le yī dùn mà	get a scolding
饱餐一顿	bǎo cān yī dùn	have a big meal; eat and drink one's fill
一顿美餐	yī dùn měi cān	a delicious meal
一顿臭骂	yī dùn chòu mà	A scolding

The new HSK (Chinese Proficiency Test) Introduction:

The new HSK (Chinese Proficiency Test) is an international standardized exam that tests and rates Chinese language proficiency. It assesses non-native Chinese speakers' abilities in using the Chinese language in their daily, academic and professional lives. HSK consists of six levels, namely the HSK (level I), HSK (level II), HSK (level III), HSK (level IV), HSK (level V), and HSK (level VI).

II. Test Levels

New HSK	Vocabulary
HSK (Level I)	150
HSK (Level II)	300
HSK (Level III)	600
HSK (Level IV)	1200
HSK (Level V)	2500
HSK (Level VI)	Over 5,000

7. Test takers who are able to pass the HSK (Level I) can understand and use very simple Chinese words and phrases, meet basic needs for communication and possess the ability to further their Chinese language studies.

8. Test takers who are able to pass the HSK (Level II) have an excellent grasp of basic Chinese and can communicate in simple and routine tasks requiring a simple and direct exchange of information on familiar and routine matters.

9. Test takers who are able to pass the HSK (Level III) can communicate in Chinese at a basic level in their daily, academic and professional lives. They can manage most communication in Chinese when travelling in China.

10. Test takers who are able to pass the HSK (Level IV) can converse in Chinese on a wide range of topics and are able to communicate fluently with native Chinese speakers.

11. Test takers who are able to pass the HSK (Level V) can read Chinese newspapers and magazines, enjoy Chinese films and plays, and give a full-length speech in Chinese.

12. Test takers who are able to pass the HSK (Level VI) can easily comprehend written and spoken information in Chinese and can effectively express themselves in Chinese, both orally and on paper.

The levels of the new HSK correspond to the levels of the Chinese Language Proficiency Scales for Speakers of Other Languages (CLPS) and the Common European Framework of Reference for Languages (CEF), GCSE, IGCSE, AS, A Level (A1, A2), IB, SAT, AP as follows:

New HSK	Vocabulary	CLPS	CEF	GCSE/IGCSE	AS, A Level (A1, A2)	IB (SL)	IB (HL)	SAT	AP
HSK (Level VI)	Over 5,000	Level V	C2				5000		
HSK (Level V)	2500		C1		2500	2500	2500	2500	2500
HSK (Level IV)	1200	Level IV	B2	1200	1200	1200	1200	1200	1200
HSK (Level III)	600	Level III	B1	600	600	600	600	600	600
HSK (Level II)	300	Level II	A2	300	300	300	300	300	300
HSK (Level I)	150	Level I	A1	150	150	150	150	150	150

The HSK (Level V) assesses test takers' abilities in the application of everyday Chinese. It is the counterpart of the Level V of the Chinese Language Proficiency Scales for Speakers of Other Languages and the C1 Level of the Common European Framework of Reference (CEF). Test takers who are able to pass the HSK (Level V) can read Chinese newspapers and magazines, enjoy Chinese films and plays and give a full-length speech in Chinese.

I. Test Target

The HSK (Level V) is intended for students who have studied Chinese 2-4 class hours per week for more than two academic years. These students have mastered 2,500 commonly used words and related grammar patterns.

II. Test Content

The HSK (Level V) test is made up of listening comprehension, reading comprehension and writing sections and contains a total of 100 items.

Section		Number of Items		Duration (Min)
I. Listening	Part I	20	45	About 30
	Part II	25		
Filling out the answer sheet(Mark your answers for listening comprehension on Answer Sheet)				5
II. Reading	Part I	15	45	45
	Part II	10		
	Part III	20		
III. Writing	Part I	8	10	40
	Part II	2		
Total	/	100		About 120

The test will last for 125 minutes in total (including 5 minutes in which the test takers fill in personal information).

David YAO, Founder of

https://edeo.biz/shop   &   www.legoomandarin.com

21 March 2019

Vocabularies Arranged Attributes and Levels

1 Noun 名词 míngcí

HSK 1 Nouns 名词 (63[3])

家	jiā	(名)[4]	family
学校	xuéxiào	(名)	school
饭馆	fànguǎn	(名)	restaurant .
商店	shāngdiàn	(名)	shop; Store
医院	yīyuàn	(名)	hospital:
火车站	huǒchē zhàn	(名)	railway station.
中国	zhōngguó	(名)	China
北京	běijīng	(名)	Beijing (Peking)

---

[3] 63 indicates the total number 63 Noun (名词) in this level HSK 1.

[4] (名) indicates 名词 míngcí Noun

上	shàng	(名) upper; upward; top
下	xià	(名) down; under; below:
前面	qiánmiàn	(名) in front; ahead:
后面	hòumiàn	(名) at the back; in the rear; behind
里	lǐ	(名) inside:
天天	tiāntiān	(名) every day
今天	jīntiān	(名) today:
明天	míngtiān	(名) tomorrow.
昨天	zuótiān	(名) yesterday
上午	shàngwǔ	(名) forenoon; Morning

中午	zhōngwǔ	(名) noon; Midday
下午	xiàwǔ	(名) afternoon
年	nián	(名) year:
月	yuè	(名) month:
日	rì	(名) day
星期	xīngqí	(名) week:
点	diǎn	(名) [used to indicate time] : o'clock
分钟	yī fēnzhōng	(名) one minute
现在	xiànzài	(名) now; Today; at present
时候	shíhòu	(名) (the duration of) time, (normally used

together with other word to form a new phrase)

| 爸爸 | bàba | (名) papa; Dad; father |
| 妈妈 | māmā | (名) mama; Mum mummy; mother |

儿子	érzi	(名) son
女儿	nǚ'ér	(名) daughter; Girl
老师	lǎoshī	(名) teacher
学生	xuéshēng	(名) pupil; Student
同学	tóngxué	(名) fellow student; Schoolmate; classmate
朋友	péngyǒu	(名) friend:
医生	yīshēng	(名) (medical) doctor:
先生	xiānshēng	(名) mister (Mr.); Gentleman; sir
小姐	xiǎojiě	(名) Miss
衣服	yīfú	(名) clothing; Clothes
水	shuǐ	(名) water
菜	cài	(名) vegetable:
米饭	mǐfàn	(名) cooked rice

水果	shuǐguǒ	(名) fruit
苹果	píngguǒ	(名) apple
茶	chá	(名) tea
杯子	bēizi	(名) cup; Glass
钱	qián	(名) money:
飞机	fēijī	(名) aircraft; aero plane; plane:
出租车	chūzū chē	(名) taxicab; Taxi
电视	diànshì	(名) television; TV:
电脑	diànnǎo	(名) computer
电影	diànyǐng	(名) film; Movie:
天气	tiānqì	(名) weather:
猫	māo	(名) cat:
狗	gǒu	(名) dog
东西	dōngxī	(名) thing (an object; something that is not living)

人	rén	(名) human being; Man; person; people
名字	míngzì	(名) name
书	shū	(名) book
汉语	hànyǔ	(名) Chinese (language)
字	zì	(名) character; Word:
桌	zhuō	(名) table; Desk:
椅子	yǐzi	(名) chair

HSK 2 Nouns 名词 (52)

公司	gōngsī	(名)[5] company; firm; corporation
机场	jīchǎng	(名 airport; airfield; aerodrome
教室	jiàoshì	(名) classroom; schoolroom

---

[5](名) indicates 名词 míngcí Noun

房间　　　　　fángjiān　　　　　　(名) room.

路　　　　　lù　　　　　　1 (名) road; path; way:

上　　　　　shàng　　　　　　(形) upper; upward; top

下　　　　　xià　　　　　　1⁶ (名) down; under; below:

---

[6] The number 1 here indicates the First meaning. One Chines Character may have many meanings. A phrase can related to many meanings. This is the hard part of Chinese language. So, pay attention to the Shape of Chinese Characters, at least you can read out or know the meaning, will help you a lot in your Chinese learning journey. i.e 请　qǐng　　1 (动) treat

请客　qǐngkè play the host; stand treat

请　　qǐng　　2 (敬) please:

请坐　qǐng zuò　　(动) Please sit; Please take a seat

请　　qǐng　　hire

聘请　pìnqǐng　　(动) invite; hire

请　　Qǐng　　3.(招待; 款待) entertain

我们请朋友吃午饭。　　wǒmen qǐng péngyǒu chī wǔfàn.　　we entertained friends to lunch.

请　　Qǐng　　4.[敬] (用于希望对方做某事) please

前面	qiánmiàn	1 (名) in front; ahead:
后面	hòumiàn	1 (名) at the back; in the rear; behind
里	lǐ	(名) 5 inside:
左边	zuǒbiān	(名) on the left.
右边	yòubiān	(名) the right (or righthand) side; the right
外	wài	(名) outside :
旁边	pángbiān	(名) side; beside
早上	zǎoshang	(名) early morning
晚上	wǎnshàng	(名) evening

请安静。	qǐng ānjìng.	be quiet, please.

小时	xiǎoshí	(名) hour
时间	shíjiān	1 (名) (the concept of) time:
去年	qùnián	last year.
号	Hào	(名) 7 date:
生日	shēng rì	(名) birthday
哥哥	gēgē	(名) (elder) brother
姐姐	jiějiě	(名) elder sister; sister
弟弟	dìdì	(名) younger brother.
妹妹	mèimei	(名) younger sister; sister
丈夫	zhàngfū	(名) husband

妻子	qī zi	(名) wife	
孩子	háizi	1(名) child:	
男人	nánrén	(名) man; husband	
女人	nǚrén	(名) woman; womenfolk	
服务员	fúwùyuán	(名) attendant; waiter; steward; stew	
鱼	yú	(名) fish	
羊肉	yángròu	(名) mutton	
牛奶	niúnǎi	(名) milk	
鸡蛋	jīdàn	(名) (hen's) egg:	

西瓜　　　xīguā　　　(名) watermelon:

咖啡　　　kāfēi　　　(名) coffee:

自行车　　　zìxíngchē　　　(名) bicycle; bike

船　　　chuán　　　(名) boat; ship:

雪　　　xuě　　　1 (名) snow

药　　　yào　　　1 (名) medicine; drug; remedy:

手机　　　shǒujī　　　(名) mobile phone

手表　　　shǒubiǎo　　　(wrist) watch

眼睛　　　yǎnjīng　　　(名) eye

身体　　　shēntǐ　　　1 (名) body

公共汽车	gōnggòng qìchē	(名) bus
报纸	bàozhǐ	(名) 1 newspaper
门	mén	1 (名) door; gate; entranc e:
题	tí	1 (名) topic; subject; title; problem:
课	kè	(名) 2 class:
姓	xìng	(名) surname; family name
问题	wèntí	1 (名) question; problem; issue:
事情	shìqíng	(名) affair; matter; thing; business:

考试	kǎoshì	(名) examination; test
票	piào	1 (名) ticket:
意思	yìsi	1 (名) meaning; idea:
颜色	yánsè	1 (名) (口) colour

HSK 3 Nouns 名词 (144)

灯	dēng	(名) lamp ;light. HSK 3 new
地方	dìfāng	(名) 1 place:
地铁	dìtiě	(名) Subway
地图	dìtú	(名) map
电梯	diàntī	(名) lift; elevator
电子邮件	diànzǐ yóujiàn	(名) E-mail
东	dōng	(名) 1 east:
冬天	dōngtiān	(名) winter
动物	dòngwù	(名) animal:

段	duàn	(名) section; part:
耳朵	ěrduǒ	(名) ear
分	Fēn	7 (名) (of time or degree) minute (= 1/60 of an hour or degree)
附近	fùjìn	(名) nearby; neighbouring; in the vicinity:
感冒	gǎnmào	(名) cold; flu:
刚才	gāngcái	(名) Just now; a moment ago:
根据	gēnjù	1 (动) on the basis of; according to :
		2 (名) basis; grounds:

这话有根据吗?

zhè huà yǒu gēnjù ma?

Is this statement based on facts?

公园	gōngyuán	(名) park
故事	gùshì	(名) 1 story; tale:
刮风	guā fēng	(名) (动) blow; blowing
关系	guānxì	1 (名) 1 relation; relationship:

国家	guójiā	(名) country; state; nation
果汁	guǒzhī	(名) fruit juice
过去	Guòqù	1 (名) past; former; previous:
河	hé	(名) river
黑板	hēibǎn	(名) blackboard
护照	hùzhào	(名) passport:
花	huā	1 (名) flower; blossom; bloom:
花园	huāyuán	(名) flower garden; garden
画	huà	1 (动) draw; paint:
环境	huánjìng	(名) environment; surroundings; circumstances:
黄	huáng	1 (形) yellow; sallow
会议	huìyì	(名) meeting; conference:
机会	jīhuì	(名) opportunity .
季节	jìjié	(名) season:
健康	jiànkāng	1 (名) health; physique: 2 (形) healthy; sound:
班	bān	(名) 1 class; team:

角	jiǎo	(名) 4 corner:
脚	jiǎo	1 (名) foot:
街道	jiēdào	1 (名) street
结婚	jiéhūn	(动) marry; get married:
节目	jiémù	(名) programme; item (on a programme); number:
节日	jiérì	(名) festival; red-letter day; holiday:
经理	jīnglǐ	2 (名) manager; director
句子	jùzi	(名) sentence:
决定	juédìng	2 (名) decision; resolution:
半	bàn	(名) half; semi- :
办法	bànfǎ	(名) way; means; measure; ways and means:
刻	kè	(名) a quarter (of an hour)
客人	kèrén	1 (名) visitor; guest
空调	kòngtiáo	1 (名) air-conditioning
口	kǒu	1 (名) 1 mouth

裤子	kùzi	(名) trousers; pants:
办公室	bàngōngshì	(名) office

筷子	kuàizi	(名) chopsticks
蓝	lán	(名) blue
礼物	lǐwù	(名) gift; present
历史	lìshǐ	(名) history; past records:
脸	liǎn	(名) face:
练习	liànxí	2 (名) exerclse
邻居	línjū	(名) neighbour:
楼	lóu	1 (名) a storeyed building:
绿	lǜ	(名) green:
马	Mǎ	(名) horse:
帽子	màozi	1 (名) hat; cap; headgear
米	mǐ	3 (名) metre; (名) rice; grain
面包	miànbāo	(名) bread:

面条	miàntiáo	(名) noodles
鼻子	bízi	(名) nose:
奶奶	nǎinai	(名) (paternal) grandmother
南	nán	(名) south
年级	niánjí	(名) grade (in school):
鸟	niǎo	(名) bird

比赛	bǐsài	(名) match; competition:
盘子	pánzi	(名) tray; plate; dish
啤酒	píjiǔ	(名) beer
葡萄	pútáo	(名) grape

普通话 pǔtōnghuà (名) Putonghua; common speech (of the Chinese language); standard Chinese pronunciation.

铅笔	qiānbǐ	(名) pencil
秋	qiū	1 (名) autumn:
裙子	qúnzi	(名) skirt
热情	rèqíng	(名) enthusiasm
别人	biérén	(名) other people; others; people :

宾馆	bīnguǎn	(名) guesthouse
伞	sǎn	1 (名) umbrella
冰箱	bīngxiāng	(名) icebox; refrigerator freezer
声音	shēngyīn	(名) sound; voice
世界	shìjiè	(名) world:
叔叔	shūshu	1 (名) father' s younger brother; uncle
树	shù	1 (名) tree:
数学	shùxué	(名) mathematics
北方	běifāng	(名) 1 north
司机	sījī	(名) driver; chauffeur
太阳	tàiyáng	1 (名) the sun:
糖	táng	1 (名) sugar: 2 sweets; candy
体育	tǐyù	(名) physical culture; physical training; sports:
同事	tóngshì	2 (名) colleague; fellow worker:
头发	tóufà	(名) hair (on the human head):

图书馆	túshū guǎn	(名) library
腿	tuǐ	1 (名) leg:
文化	wénhuà	1 (名) civilization; culture
西	xī	(名) west
习惯	xíguàn	2 (名) habit; custom:
洗手间	xǐshǒujiān	(名) toilet; lavatory; washroom; rest room
夏	xià	(名) summer
香蕉	xiāngjiāo	(名) banana
校长	xiàozhǎng	(名) head of a school (headmaster, principal, president, chancellor)

鞋	xié	(名) shoes
新闻	xīnwén	(名) news:
信	xìn	1 (名) letter:
行李箱	xínglǐ xiāng	(名) luggage case or trunk; baggage
兴趣	xìngqù	(名) interest:
熊猫	xióngmāo	(名) panda
眼镜	yǎnjìng	(名) glasses; spectacles

要求	yāoqiú	(名) requirements; demands
爷爷	yéyé	1 (名) (口) (paternal) grandfather
一会儿	yīhuǐ'er	1 (名) a little while
以后	yǐhòu	(名) after; afterwards; later; hereafter:
以前	yǐqián	(名) before; formerly; previously:
音乐	yīnyuè	(名) music:
银行	yínháng	(名) bank
游戏	yóuxì	(名) recreation; game:
菜单	càidān	(名) menu
月亮	yuèliàng	(名) the moon
云	yún	2 (名) cloud
草	cǎo	1 (名) grass; straw
层	céng	(名) 2 storey; floor:
站	zhàn	(名) station; stop:

照片	zhàopiàn	(名) photograph; picture:
照相机	zhàoxiàngjī	(名) camera
中间	zhōngjiān	1 (名) among; between:
周末	zhōumò	(名) weekend
字典	zìdiǎn	(名) dictionary
最近	zuìjìn	1 (名) recently; lately; of late:
作业	zuòyè	1 (名) school assignment:

超市	chāoshì	(名) supermarket
作用	zuòyòng	1 (名) role; function:
衬衫	chènshān	(名) shirt
成绩	chéngjī	(名) achievement; success:
城市	chéng shì	(名) town; city
厨房	chúfáng	(名) kitchen:
春	chūn	1 (名) spring:
词语	cíyǔ	(名) words and expressions; phrase; general term including monosyllables through to short phrases
蛋糕	dàngāo	(名) cake

| 行李 | xínglǐ | (名) luggage; baggage: |

HSK 4 Nouns 名词 (230)

爱情	àiqíng	(名) love (between man and woman)
安全	ānquán	(名) safe; Secure:
表格	biǎogé	(名) form; Table:
标准	biāozhǔn	(名) standard; Criterion
笔记本	bǐjìběn	(名) notebook
饼干	bǐnggān	(名) biscuit; Cracker
博士	bóshì	(名) PhD doctor
部分	bùfèn	(名) part; Section; share:
材料	cáiliào	(名) material; Data:
长城	chángchéng	(名) the Great Wall
长江	chángjiāng	(名) the Changjiang (Yangtze) River
窗户	chuānghù	(名) opening in a wall for letting in air and light; Window
传真	chuánzhēn	(名) facsimile; Fax:
词典	cídiǎn	(名) dictionary; Lexicon
答案	dá'àn	(名) answer; Solution;

大夫	dàifū	(名) doctor; Physician
代表	dàibiǎo	(名) representative; Deputy; delegate 2 (动) represent; Stand for:
当地	dāngdì	(名) in the locality; Local:
当时	dāngshí	(名) then; At that time
刀	dāo	(名) knife; Sword:
到处	dàochù	(名) at all places; Everywhere:
导游	dǎoyóu	(名) tourist guide
大使馆	dàshǐ guǎn	(名) embassy
底	dǐ	(名) bottom; Base
地球	dìqiú	(名) the earth; The globe:
地址	dìzhǐ	(名) address
动作	dòngzuò	(名) movement; Action:
堵车	dǔchē	(名) Traffic jam
对话	duìhuà	(名) dialogue
对面	duìmiàn	(名) opposite:
肚子	dùzi	(名) triple; Stomach; belly
儿童	értóng	(名) children
法律	fǎlǜ	(名) law:
方法	fāngfǎ	(名) method; way; means
方面	fāngmiàn	(名) aspect; respect; side:
方向	fāngxiàng	(名) direction; orientation :

烦恼	fánnǎo	(名) Annoyance; worries 2 (形) worried; vexed:
范围	fànwéi	(名) scope; Limits; range
风景	fēngjǐng	(名) scenery; Landscape
父亲	fùqīn	(名) father
感觉	gǎnjué	(名) feeling; sense; perception; sensation 2 (动) feel; sense; perceive
感情	gǎnqíng	(名) feelings; Emotion; sentiment:
个子	gèzi	(名) height; stature; build
工具	gōngjù	(名) tool; instrument:
公里	gōnglǐ	(名) kilometer (km)
工资	gōngzī	(名) wages; Salary:
光	guāng	(名) light; ray:
广播	guǎngbò	(名) broadcasting 2 (动) broadcast
广告	guǎnggào	(名) advertisement:
关键	guānjiàn	(名) key; Crux
管理	guǎnlǐ	(名) management (动) manage; Administer; run
观众	guānzhòng	(名) audience; spectator; viewer
规定	guīdìng	(名) rule; Stipulation 1 (动) stipulate:
顾客	gùkè	(名) customer; client
过程	guòchéng	(名) process; course
海洋	hǎiyáng	(名) seas and oceans; ocean:
汗	hàn	(名) sweat; perspiration:

航班	hángbān	(名) scheduled flight; flight number
寒假	hánjià	(名) winter vacation (or holidays)
好处	hǎochù	(名) benefit; advantage:
号码	hàomǎ	(名) number:
盒子	hé zi	(名) box; case:
后来	hòulái	(名) af terwards; la ter
猴子	hóu zi	(名) monkey
回忆 recall :	Huíyì	(名) memoirs; reminiscences (动) call to mind; recollect;
火	huǒ	(名) fire:
活动	huódòng	(名) activity; maneuver 2 (动) move about: exercise:
护士	hùshì	(名) (hospital) nurse
价格	jiàgé	(名) price:
家具	jiājù	(名) furniture:
奖金	jiǎngjīn	(名) money award; bonus; premium
将来	jiānglái	(名) future:
交流	jiāoliú	(名) exchange; interflow; interchange:
教授	jiàoshòu	(名) professor:
交通	jiāotōng	(名) traffic; Communications:
教育	jiàoyù	(名) education:
饺子 ravioli	jiǎozi	(名) dumpling (with meat and vegetable stuffing); jiaozi;
加油站	jiāyóu zhàn	(名) filling (or petrol, gas) station

基础	jīchǔ	(名) foundation; base
结果	jiéguǒ	(名) result; outcome
计划	jìhuà	(名) plan; project; programme:
警察	jǐngchá	(名) police; policeman:
经济	jīngjì	(名) economy:
京剧	jīngjù	(名) Beijing opera
经历	jīnglì	(名) experience:
精神	jīngshén	(名) spirit; mind; consciousness :
经验	jīngyàn	(名) experience:
竞争	jìngzhēng	(名) competition (动) compete:
镜子	jìngzi	(名) mirror.
技术	jìshù	(名) technology; skill ; technique:
记者	jìzhě	(名) reporter; correspondent; newsman; journalist:
距离	jùlí	(名) , distance:
看法	kànfǎ	(名) a way of looking at things; view
科学	kēxué	(名 science; scientific knowledge:
空气	kōngqì	(名) air:
困难	kùnnán	(名) difficulty:
老虎	lǎohǔ	(名) tiger
垃圾桶	lā jī tǒng	(名) Trash can; Rubbish bin
礼貌	lǐmào	(名) courtesy; manners:
力气	lìqì	(名) physical strength; effort:

理想	lǐxiǎng	(名) ideal; dream:
律师	lùshī	(名) lawyer; (英) barrister; (英)solicitor; (美) attorney
麻烦	máfan	(名) trouble 2 (形) troublesome; inconvenient:
毛巾	máojīn	(名) towel
梦	mèng	(名) dream:
密码	mìmǎ	(名) cipher; secret code; password; passcode
民族	mínzú	(名) nation; nationality:
目的	mùdì	(名) purpose; aim; goal; objective; end:
母亲	mǔqīn	(名) mother
耐心	nàixīn	(名) patience 2 (形) patient:
内	nèi	(名) inside; inner part or side:
内容	nèiróng	(名) content:
能力	néng lì	(名) ability; capability.
年龄	niánlíng	(名) age
农村	nóngcūn	(名) rural area; countryside:
皮肤	pífū	(名) skin
乒乓球	pīngpāng qiú	(名) Table-tennis
平时	píngshí	(名) in normal times
瓶子	píngzi	(名) bottle; jar; vase:
脾气	píqì	(名) temperament; disposition:
墙	Qiáng	(名)wall:
签证	qiānzhèng	(名) visa:

桥	qiáo	(名) bridge
巧克力	qiǎokèlì	(名) chocolate
气候	qìhòu	(名) climate:
情况	qíngkuàng	(名) situation; condition; state of affairs:
亲戚	qīnqī	(名) relative
其中	qízhōng	(名) among whom; among which:
缺点	Quēdiǎn	(名) shortcoming; weakness; defect
群	qún	(名) group; herd; flock:
人民币	rénmínbì	(名) Renmin bi (RMB) , currency of the People's Republic of China
任务	rènwù	(名) task; mission; assignment
日记	rìjì	(名) diary:
入口	rùkǒu	(名) entrance.
森林	sēnlín	(名) forest:
沙发	shāfā	(名) sofa
社会	shèhuì	(名) society:
省	shěng	(名) province
生活	shēnghuó	(名) life:
生命	shēngmìng	(名) life:
申请	shēnqǐng	(名) application(动) apply for :
失败	shībài	(名) failure; defeat
市场	shìchǎng	(名) marketplace; market; bazaar:

师傅	shīfù	(名) master worker
世纪	shìjì	(名) century
食品	shípǐn	(名) foodstuff; food; provisions:
狮子	shīzi	(名) lion
首都	shǒudū	(名) capital (of a country)
售货员	shòuhuòyuán	(名) shop assistant; salesclerk :
收入	shōurù	(名) income; revenue; earnings:
数量	shùliàng	(名) quantity; amount
顺序	shùnxù	(名) sequence; order
硕士	shuòshì	(名) Master:
数字	shùzì	(名) numeral; figure; digit:
酸	suān	(名) acid 2 (形) sour; tart:
速度	sùdù	(名) speed; velocity
塑料袋	sùliào dài	(名) plastic bag.
孙子	sūnzi	(名) grandson
台	tái	(名) table; desk:
态度	tàidù	(名) manner; bearing; how one conducts oneself:
汤	tāng	(名) soup; broth:
讨论	tǎolùn	(名) discussion (动) discuss; talk over:
特点	tèdiǎn	(名) characteristic; special feature; peculiarity
条件	tiáojiàn	(名) condition; term; factor:

通知	tōngzhī	(名) notice ; circular 2 (动) notify; inform :
网球	wǎngqiú	(名) tennis
网站	wǎngzhàn	(名) web site
袜子	Wàzi	(名) socks; stockings
味道	wèidào	(名) taste; flavor:
温度	wēndù	(名) temperature.
文章	wénzhāng	(名) essay; article
污染	wūrǎn	(名) pollution.
现代	xiàndài	(名) modern times; the contemporary age
效果	xiàoguǒ	(名) effect; result:
笑话	xiàohuà	(名) joke:
小说	xiǎoshuō	(名) novel; fiction:
消息	xiāoxī	(名) news; information:
西红柿	xīhóngshì	(名) tomato
性别	xìngbié	(名) Gender; sexual distinction; sex:
幸福	xìngfú	(名) happiness; Well-being
性格	xìnggé	(名) nature; character; temperament
心情	xīnqíng	(名) state of mind; mood:
信心	xìnxīn	(名) confidence; faith
信用卡	xìnyòngkǎ	(名) credit card
洗衣机	xǐyījī	(名) washing machine.
血	xuè	(名) blood

牙膏	yágāo	(名) toothpaste
压力	yālì	(名) pressure:
盐	yán	(名) salt:
阳光	yángguāng	(名) sunlight.
样子	yàngzi	(名) appearance; shape
研究生	yánjiūshēng	(名) postgraduate.
演员	yǎnyuán	(名) actor or actress; ballet dancer or acrobatic performer
钥匙	yàoshi	(名) key:
亚洲	yàzhōu	(名) Asia
页	yè	(名) leaf; page:
叶子	yèzi	(名) leaf
意见	yìjiàn	(名) idea; view; opinion:
饮料	yǐnliào	(名) drink; beverage
印象	yìnxiàng	(名) impression:
艺术	yìshù	(名) art :
优点	yōudiǎn	(名) strong point.
友好	yǒuhǎo	(名) close friend; friend
友谊	yǒuyì	(名) friendship:
原因	yuányīn	(名) cause; reason:

语法	yǔfǎ	(名) grammar
羽毛球	yǔmáoqiú	(名) badminton
语言	yǔyán	(名) language:
杂志	zázhì	(名) magazine
责任	zérèn	(名) duty; responsibility:
质量	zhìliàng	(名) quality
知识	zhīshì	(名) knowledge:
植物	zhíwù	(名) plant; flora:
职业	zhíyè	(名) occupatlon :
重点	zhòngdiǎn	(名) focal point; emphasis:
中文	zhōngwén	(名) the Chinese language
周围	zhōuwéi	(名) around ; round ; about:
猪	zhū	(名) pig; hog; swine:
专业	zhuānyè	(名) special field of study; major
主动	zhǔdòng	(名) initiative:
主意	zhǔyì	(名) idea; plan; decision:
自然	zìrán	(名) nature 2 (副) in due course; naturally
嘴	zuǐ	(名) mouth:
最后	Zuìhòu	(名) last; final; at last; eventually:
座位	zuòwèi	(名) seat
作者	zuòzhě	(名) author; writer
组织	zǔzhī	(名) organization 2 (动) organize

约会	yuēhuì	(名) appomtment; engagement; date; rendezvous:

HSK 5 Nouns 名词 (571)

家	jiā	(名)[7] family
朝	cháo	(名) dynasty:
大象	dà xiàng	(名) elephant
领域	lǐngyù	(名) territory; domain
语气	yǔqì	(名) tone; manner of speaking:
舅舅	jiùjiu	(名) uncle (mother's brother)
老百姓	lǎobǎixìng	(名) (口) common people; ordinary people; civilians
球迷	qiúmí	(名) (ball game) fan:
内科	nèikē	(名) (department of internal medicine:
戒指	jièzhǐ	(名) (finger) ring
姥姥	lǎolao	(名) (maternal) grandmother; grandma

[7](名) indicates 名词 míngcí Noun

软件	ruǎnjiàn	(名) (of computers) software
作文	zuòwén	(名) (student's) composition; essay
蜡烛	làzhú	(名) (wax) candle
窗帘	chuānglián	(名) (window) curtain
土豆	tǔdòu	(名) (口) potato
光临	guānglín	(名) (敬) gracious presence (of a guest, etc.):
女士	nǚshì	(名) [polite form of address for women]:
钟	zhōng	(名) 1 bell 2 clock
立方	lìfāng	(名) 1 cube:
餐厅	cāntīng	(名) 1 dining room 2 restaurant
常识	chángshì	(名) 1 general knowledge 2 common sense
手套	shǒutào	(名) 1 gloves; mittens 2 baseball gloves; mitts
程序	chéngxù	(名) 1 order; procedure; course:
道理	dàolǐ	(名) 1 principle; truth
比例	bǐlì	(名) 1 ratio; proportion 2 scale
角色	juésè	(名) 1 role; part: 2 type of role (in traditional Chinese drarma)
根	Gēn	(名) 1 root; 2 cause; origin; source; foot

位置	wèizhì	(名) 1 seat; place 2 poisition
待遇	dàiyù	(名) 1 treatment 2 pay, wages, salary
公元	gōngyuán	(名) A . D.; the Christian era:
讲座	jiǎngzuò)	(名) a course of lectures; series of lectures
台阶	táijiē	(名) a flight of steps; stairs
华裔	huáyì	(名) a person of Chinese descent
人才	réncái	(名) a person of talent
口味	kǒuwèi	(名) a person's taste:
学术	xuéshù	(名) academic research:
意外	yìwài	(名) accident; mishap:
账户	zhànghù	(名) account:
会计	kuàijì	(名) accounting; accountant
成就	chéngjiù	(名) achievement; accomplishment; attainment; success
行动	xíngdòng	(名) action; operation:
年纪	niánjì	(名) age:
年代	niándài	(名) age; years; time:
农业	nóngyè	(名) agriculture; farming:

一辈子	yībèizi	(名) all one's life; a lifetime
过敏	guòmǐn	(名) allergy
救护车	jiùhù chē	(名) ambulance.
娱乐	yúlè	(名) amusement; entertainment; recreation:
古代	gǔdài	(名) ancient times.
公寓	gōngyù	(名) apartment house; block of flats
面积	miànjī	(名) area:
地区	dìqū	(名) area; district; region:
胳膊	gēbó	(名) arm:
目前	mùqián	(名) at present; at the moment:
同时	tóngshí	(名) at the same time; simultaneously; meanwhile; in the meantime:
气氛	qìfēn	(名) atmosphere:
姑姑	gūgū	(名) aunt (father's sister)
背景	bèijǐng	(名) background; backdrop:
平衡	pínghéng	(名) balance; equilibrium:
阳台	yángtái	(名) balcony
竹子	zhúzi	(名) bamboo:

岸	àn	(名) bank; shore; coast:
宴会	yànhuì	(名) banquet; feast; dinner party
酒吧	jiǔbā	(名) bar; pub
日用品	rìyòngpǐn	(名) basic commodities
盆	pén	(名) basin; tub; pot:
电池	diànchí	(名) battery
豆腐	dòufu	(名) bean curd
胡须	húxū	(名) beard, moustache or whiskers
卧室	wòshì	(名) bedroom
从前	cóngqián	(名) before; in the past; formerly:
行为	xíngwéi	(名) behaviour; conduct; action:
铃	líng	(名) bell:
零食	língshí	(名) between-meal nibbles; snacks
简历	jiǎnlì	(名) biographical notes; resumé; curriculum vitae (cv)
登机牌	dēng jī pái	(名) boarding pass
骨头	gǔtou	(名) bone:
书架	shūjià	(名) bookshelves
老板	lǎobǎn	(名) boss; shopkeeper; proprietor

双方	shuāngfāng	(名) both sides; the two parties:
对象	duìxiàng	(名) boy or girl friend
品种	pǐnzhǒng	(名) breed; variety:
兄弟	xiōngdì	(名) brothers:
蝴蝶	húdié	(名) butterfly
目录	mùlù	(名) ca talogue; list:
灾害	zāihài	(名) calamity; disaster.
日历	rìlì	(名) calendar
字幕	zìmù	(名) caption (of film, video, etc.); subtitles
爱心	Àixīn	(名) Caring heart; Thoughts and feelings of caring, love of others
地毯	dìtǎn	(名) carpet; rug
动画片	dònghuà piàn	(名) cartoon movie
套	tào	(名) case; cover:
现金	xiànjīn	(名) cash:
缘故	yuángù	(名) cause; reason
中心	zhōngxīn	(名) center.
总裁	zǒngcái	(名) CEO; chairman

主席	zhǔxí	(名) chairman ; chairperson:
冠军	guànjūn	(名) champion
特征	tèzhēng	(名) characteristic; feature; trait
充电器	chōngdiàn qì	(名) charger
化学	huàxué	(名) chemistry:
支票	zhīpiào	(名) cheque; check:
胸	xiōng	(名) chest; bosom
辣椒	làjiāo	(名) chilli; red pepper
象棋	xiàngqí	(名) Chinese chess
圈	quān	(名) circle; ring:
文明	wénmíng	(名) civilization; culture 2 (形) civilized:
经典	jīngdiǎn	(名) classics
夹子	jiázi	(名) clip; tongs:
布	bù	(名) cloth
俱乐部	jùlèbù	(名) club
教练	jiàoliàn	(名) coach; instructor:
煤炭	méitàn	(名) coal
硬币	yìngbì	(名) coin; specie

集体	jítǐ	(名) collective:
梳子	shūzi	(名) comb
未来	wèilái	(名) coming; approaching; next; future :
商业	shāngyè	(名) commerce ; trade; business:
商品	shāngpǐn	(名) commodity; goods; merchandise:
通讯	tōngxùn	(名) communication:
成分	chéngfèn	(名) composition; component part; ingredient:
概念	gàiniàn	(名) concept; notion; idea
结论	jiélùn	(名) conclusion (of a syllogism)
状况	zhuàngkuàng	(名) condition; state:
作为	zuòwéi	(名) conduct; action:
后果	hòuguǒ	(名) consequence; aftermath:
合同	hétóng	(名) contract:
矛盾	máodùn	(名) contradiction:
铜	tóng	(名) copper (Cu)
费用	fèiyòng	(名) cost; expenses; expenditure:
价值	jiàzhí	(名) cost; value
棉花	miánhuā	(名) cotton:

县	xiàn	(名) county
勇气	yǒngqì	(名) courage ; nerve
课程	kèchéng	(名) coursc; curriculum:
法院	fǎyuàn	(名) court of justice; law court; court:
胆小鬼	dǎnxiǎoguǐ	(名) coward
证件	zhèngjiàn	(名) credentials; certificate; papers
罪犯	zuìfàn	(名) criminal; culprit
黄瓜	huángguā	(名) cucumber
海关	hǎiguān	(名) customs house; customs:
数据	shùjù	(名) data;
日期	rìqí	(名) date:
残疾	cánjí	(名) deformity:
角度	jiǎodù	(名) degree of an angle
民主	mínzhǔ	(名) democracy
部门	bùmén	(名) department; branch:
沙漠	shāmò	(名) desert
愿望	yuànwàng	(名) desire; wish; aspiration:
命运	mìngyùn	(名) destiny; fate; lot :

细节	xìjié	(名) details
决心	juéxīn	(名) determination; resolution:
露	lù	(名) dew
差别	chābié	(名) difference; disparity:
外交	wàijiāo	(名) diplomacy; foreign affairs:
纪律	jìlǜ	(名) discipline:
文件	wénjiàn	(名) documents; papers; instruments
宿舍	sùshè	(名) dormitory; flat
龙	lóng	(名) dragon
戏剧	xìjù	(名) drama; play
抽屉	chōutì	(名) drawer
客厅	kètīng	(名) drawing room; parlor
服装	fúzhuāng	(名) dress; garment; costume:
陆地	lùdì	(名) dry land; land
灰尘	huīchén	(名) dust; dirt:
义务	yìwù	(名) duty; obligation:
朝代	cháodài	(名) dynasty
地震	dìzhèn	(名) earthquake; seism:

效率	xiàolǜ	(名) efficiency
功夫	gōngfū	(名) effort; 2 kung fu; martial arts; (same as 工夫)
皇帝	huángdì	(名) emperor
皇后	huánghòu	(名) empress
敌人	dírén	(名) enemy; foe
能源	néngyuán	(名) energy source
精力	jīnglì	(名) energy; vigour; stamina:
工程师	gōngchéngshī	(名) engineer
企业	qǐyè	(名) enterprise; business:
信封	xìnfēng	(名) envelope
平等	píngděng	(名) equality
设备	shèbèi	(名) equipment; facilities:
本质	běnzhí	(名) essence; true nature
证据	zhèngjù	(名) evidence; proof; testimony:
试卷	shìjuàn	(名) exammation paper; test paper
汇率	huìlǜ	(名) exchange rate:
借口	jièkǒu	(名) excuse; pretext:
实验	shíyàn	(名) experiment; test:

专家	zhuānjiā	(名) expert; specialist
表现	biǎoxiàn	(名) expression ; manifestation:
表情	biǎoqíng	(名) expression:
眉毛	méimáo	(名) eyebrow; brow
事实	shìshí	(名) fact:
因素	yīnsù	(名) factor; element :
工厂	gōngchǎng	(名) factory; mill ; plant; works
家庭	jiātíng	(名) family; household:
名牌	míngpái	(名) famous brand:
扇子	shànzi	(名) fan
时尚	shí shàng	(名) Fashion; vogue
节	jié	(名) festival; red-letter day; holiday:
田野	tiányě	(名) field; open land
人物	rénwù	(名) figure; personage:
决赛	juésài	(名) finals:
美术	měishù	(名) fine arts:
手指	shǒuzhǐ	(名) finger
鞭炮	biānpào	(名) firecrackers

闪电	shǎndiàn	(名) flashes of lightning
雾	wù	(名) fog; mist; haze
食物	shíwù	(名) food
祖先	zǔxiān	(名) forefathers; ancestors
叉子	chā zi	(名) fork
形式	xíngshì	(名) form:
形状	xíngzhuàng	(名) form; appearance; shape
运气	yùnqì	(名) fortune; luck:
丁	dīng	(名) fourth 2 man:
自由	zìyóu	(名) freedom; liberty:
果实	guǒshí	(名) fruit; gains:
功能	gōngnéng	(名) function:
资金	zījīn	(名) fund:
前途	qiántú	(名) future; prospect:
车库	chēkù	(名) garage
地理	dìlǐ	(名) geography
姿势	zīshì	(名) gesture; posture; position:
姑娘	gūniáng	(名) girl

魅力	mèilì	(名) glamour; enchantment; fascination:
玻璃	bōlí	(名) glass:
光荣	guāngróng	(名) glory; honor; credit:
黄金	huángjīn	(名) gold:
政府	zhèngfǔ	(名) government
官	guān	(名) government official; officer:
班主任	bānzhǔrèn	(名) grade adviser; a teacher in charge of a class
粮食	liángshí	(名) grain; cereals; food
克	kè	(名) gram (g)
合影	héyǐng	(名) group photo (or picture)
枪	qiāng	(名) gun; rifle:
健身房	jiànshēnfáng	(名) gym
毛	máo	(名) hair; feather; down
手工	shǒugōng	(名) handwork:
硬件	yìngjiàn	(名) hardware (of a computer)
兔子	tù zi	(名) hare; rabbit:
脑袋	nǎodai	(名) head
英雄	yīngxióng	(名) hero:

洞	dòng	(名) hole; cavity; cave
家乡	jiāxiāng	(名) hometown; native place
蜜蜂	mì fēng	(名) honey-bee
嘉宾	jiābīn	(名) honored guest; welcome guest
荣誉	róngyù	(名) honour; credit :
家务	jiāwù	(名) household duties:
观念	guānniàn	(名) idea; concept
成语	chéngyǔ	(名) idiom; proverb; set phrase
幻想	huànxiǎng	(名) illusion; figment of one's imagination:
形象	xíngxiàng	(名) image; imagery:
想像 (想象)	xiǎngxiàng	(名) imagination:
一旦	yīdàn	(名) in a single day; in a very short time:
事先	shìxiān	(名) in advance ; beforehand; prior:
愤怒	fènnù	(名) indignation; anger; wrath
个性	gèxìng	(名) individual character; individuality; personality
工业	gōngyè	(名) industry:
资料	zīliào	(名) information; data
信息	xìnxī	(名) information; news:

最初	zuìchū	(名) initial; first:
设施	shèshī	(名) installation; facilities:
保险	bǎoxiǎn	(名) insurance:
利息	lìxí	(名) interest
利益	lìyì	(名) interest; benefit; profit:
中介	zhōngjiè	(名) intermediate
发票	fāpiào	(名) invoice; bill; receipt:
钢铁	gāngtiě	(名) iron and steel; steel
岛	dǎo	(名) island:
项目	xiàngmù	(名) Item; Project
牛仔裤	niúzǎikù	(名) jeans
壶	hú	(名) kettle; pot:
键盘	jiànpán	(名) keyboard; fingerboard
类	lèi	(名) kind; type; class; category:
幼儿园	yòu'éryuán	(名) kindergarten
小伙子	xiǎohuǒzi	(名) lad; young fellow
勺子	sháozi	(名) ladle; scoop
土地	tǔdì	(名) land; soil; territory

房东	fángdōng	(名) landlord
胡同	hútòng	(名) lane; alley; hutong
厕所	cèsuǒ	(名) lavatory; toilet; W. C
规律	guīlǜ	(名) law; regular pattern:
学问	xuéwèn	(名) learning; knowledge; scholarship:
皮鞋	píxié	(名) leather shoes:
程度	chéngdù	(名) level; degree; extent:
执照	zhízhào	(名) licence; permit:
盖	gài	(名) lid; cover (动) to cover
人生	rénshēng	(名) life:
寿命	shòumìng	(名) lifespan; life :
点心	diǎnxīn	(名) light refreshments; Dim Sum
液体	yètǐ	(名) liquid
文学	wénxué	(名) literature
锁	suǒ	(名) lock:
逻辑	luójí	(名) logic:
长途	chángtú	(名) long-distance:
传说	chuánshuō	(名) lore; legend:

卡车	kǎchē	(名) lorry; truck
肺	fèi	(名) lung
机器	jīqì	(名) machine; machinery; apparatus:
玉米	yùmǐ	(名) maize; corn
人类	rénlèi	(名) mankind; humanity:
婚姻	hūnyīn	(名) marriage; matrimony:
主人	zhǔrén	(名) master; owner
火柴	huǒchái	(名) match (a short, thin stick made of wood to make fire)
物质	wùzhí	(名) matter; substance; material:
意义	yìyì	(名) meaning; sense; significance:
措施	cuòshī	(名) measure; suitable action:
金属	jīnshǔ	(名) metal:
麦克风	màikèfēng	(名) microphone
军事	jūnshì	(名) military affairs:
矿泉水	kuàngquán shuǐ	(名) mineral water
奇迹	qíjī	(名) miracle; wonder:
错误	cuòwù	(名) mistake; error:

近代	jìndài	(名) modern times:
情绪	qíngxù	(名) mood; spirit; morale:
道德	dàodé	(名) morals; morality:
祖国	zǔguó	(名) motherland
高速公路	gāosù gōnglù	(名) motorway; expressway; freeway
鼠标	shǔbiāo	(名) mouse
老鼠	lǎoshǔ	(名) mouse; rat
太太	tàitài	(名) Mrs.; Madame 2 one's wife
胶水	jiāoshuǐ	(名) mucilage; glue
肌肉	jīròu	(名) muscle:
神话	shénhuà	(名) mythology; myth
名片	míngpiàn	(名) name card; visiting card; calling card; name card
解说员	jiěshuō yuán	(名) Narrator
国庆节	guóqìng jié	(名) National Day
国籍	guójí	(名) nationality
资源	zīyuán	(名) natural resources
性质	xìngzhì	(名) nature; quality:

脖子	bózi	(名) neck
项链	xiàngliàn	(名) necklace
谈判	tánpàn	(名) negotiations; talk:
神经	shénjīng	(名) nerve
元旦	yuándàn	(名) New Year's Day
除夕	Chúxì	(名) New Year's Eve
隔壁	gébì	(名) next door
夜	yè	(名) night; evening
如今	rújīn	(名) now ; nowadays:
核心	héxīn	(名) nucleus; core; kernel; the heart of the matter:
营养	yíngyǎng	(名) nutrition; nourishment:
开幕式	kāimù shì	(名) opening ceremony
对手	duìshǒu	(名) opponent; adversary
对方	duìfāng	(名) opposite side; the other party
光盘	guāngpán	(名) optical disk:
命令	mìnglìng	(名) order; command:
秩序	zhìxù	(名) order; sequence:
提纲	tígāng	(名) outline

全面	quánmiàn	(名) overall; all-round; comprehensive:
痛苦	tòngkǔ	(名) pain; suffering; agony
伙伴	huǒbàn	(名) partner; companion
和平	hépíng	(名) peace:
桃	táo	(名) peach
花生	huāshēng	(名) peanut; groundnut
梨	lí	(名) pear
农民	nóngmín	(名) peasant
行人	xíng rén	(名) pedestrian
深刻	shēnkè	(名) penetrating; profound
时期	shíqí	(名) period:
人事	rénshì	(名) personnel matters:
人员	rényuán	(名) personnel; staff:
宠物	chǒngwù	(名) pet
汽油	qìyóu	(名) petrol; gasoline; gas
小偷	xiǎotōu	(名) petty thief; pilferer; pickpocket
现象	xiànxiàng	(名) phenomenon :
哲学	zhéxué	(名) philosophy:

物理	wùlǐ	(名) physics
鸽子	gēzi	(名) pigeon; dove:
枕头	zhěntou	(名) pillow
方案	fāng'àn	(名) plan; scheme; program:
操场	cāochǎng	(名) playground; sports ground
零钱	língqián	(名) small change; change
零花钱	línghuā qián	(名) pocket money
零用钱	língyòng qián	(名) pocket money
诗	shī	(名) poetry; verse; poem
政策	zhèngcè	(名) policy.
政治	zhèngzhì	(名) politics ; political affairs:
池子	chízi	(名) pool; pond
人口	rénkǒu	(名) population:
地位	dìwèi	(名) position; status :
成果	chéngguǒ	(名) positive result; accomplishment
邮局	yóujú	(名) post office
明信片	míngxìnpiàn	(名) postcard
锅	guō	(名) pot; pan; cooker:

权力	quánlì	(名) power; authority:
力量	lìliàng	(名) power; force; strength:
实践	shíjiàn	(名) practice:
实习	shíxí	(名) practice; fieldwork; field trip:
总理	zǒnglǐ	(名) premier; prime minister
总统	zǒngtǒng	(名) president (of a republic)
王子	wángzǐ	(名) prince
公主	gōngzhǔ	(名) prince
原则	yuánzé	(名) principle:
手续	shǒuxù	(名) procedures; formalities:
产品	chǎnpǐn	(名) product; produce:
利润	lìrùn	(名) profit:
日程	rìchéng	(名) program; schedule:
财产	cáichǎn	(名) property
心理	xīnlǐ	(名) psychology; mentality:
广场	guǎngchǎng	(名) public square
标点	biāodiǎn	(名) punctuation
资格	zīgé	(名) qualifications:

疑问	yíwèn	(名) query; question; doubt:
被子	bèizi	(名) quilt (a decorative cover for a bed or cotton blanket)
车厢	chēxiāng	(名) railway carriage; railroad car
彩虹	cǎihóng	(名) rainbow
士兵	shìbīng	(名) rank-and-file soldiers; privates
原料	yuánliào	(名) raw material.
反应	fǎnyìng	(名) reaction:
现实	xiànshí	(名) realistic; practical:
理由	lǐyóu	(名) reason; ground; argument:
收据	shōujù	(名) receipt
感想	gǎnxiǎng	(名) reflections; thoughts; impressions
遗憾	yíhàn	(名) regret; pity :
宗教	zōngjiào	(名) religion:
革命	gémìng	(名) revolution
谜语	míyǔ	(名) riddle; conundrum
权利	quánlì	(名) right
风险	fēngxiǎn	(名) risk:

烤鸭	kǎoyā	(名) roast duck.
屋子	wūzi	(名) room
绳子	shéngzi	(名) rope; cord; string:
橡皮	xiàngpí	(名) rubber eraser
规矩	guījǔ	(名) rule; established practice:
规则	guīzé	(名) rule; regulation:
尺子	chǐzi	(名) ruler
柜台	guìtái	(名) sales counter:
沙滩	shātān	(名) sandy beach
规模	guīmó	(名) scale; scope; dimensions:
围巾	wéijīn	(名) scarf
情景	qíngjǐng	(名) scene; sight; circumstances:
景色	jǐngsè	(名) scenery; view; scene; landscape:
名胜古迹	míngshèng gǔjī	(名) scenic spots and historical sites
剪刀	jiǎndāo	(名) scissors; shears :
海鲜	hǎixiān	(名) seafood
乙	Yǐ	(名) second:
秘书	mìshū	(名) secretary:

连续剧	liánxùjù	(名) serial drama; serial:
影子	yǐngzi	(名) shadow; reflection:
股票	gǔpiào	(名) share; stock:
短信	duǎnxìn	(名) short message; Text messaging; SMS
肩膀	jiānbǎng	(名) shoulder
标志	biāozhì	(名) sign; mark; symbol:
信号	xìnhào	(名) signal
丝绸	isīchóu	(名) silk cloth; silk:
银	yín	(名) silver
以来	yǐlái	(名) since :
形势	xíngshì	(名) situation; circumstances
滑冰	huábīng	(名) skate; ice skating; skating:
本领	běnlǐng	(名) skill; ability; capability:
小吃	xiǎochī	(名) snack; refreshments:
蛇	shé	(名) snake; serpent
肥皂	féizào	(名) soap:
风俗	fēngsú	(名) social customs:
交际	jiāojì	(名) social intercourse; communication:

固体	gùtǐ	(名) solid:
录音	lùyīn	(名) sound recording:
酱油	jiàngyóu	(名) soy sauce; soy
空间	kōngjiān	(名) space:
零件	língjiàn	(名) spare parts; spares
业余	yèyú	(名) spare time; amateur:
平方	píngfāng	(名) square
阶段	jiēduàn	(名) stage; phase:
明星	míngxīng	(名) star:
状态	zhuàngtài	(名) state of affairs; appearance:
文具	wénjù	(名) stationery
身材	shēncái	(名) stature; figure; build
身份	shēnfèn	(名) status; capacity; identity:
馒头	mántou	(名) steamed bun; steamed bread
包子	bāo zi	(名) steamed stuffed bun
步骤	bùzhòu	(名) step; move; measure:
棒	bàng	(名) 1 stick; club; cudgel
		2 (形) strong, good, excellent

胃	wèi	(名) stomach:
石头	shítou	(名) stone; rock
结构	jiégòu	(名) structure; composition; construction:
风格	fēnggé	(名) style:
样式	yàngshì	(名) style; type .
郊区	jiāoqū	(名) suburban district; suburbs; outskirts
礼拜天	lǐbài tiān	(名) Sunday
废话	fèihuà	(名) superfluous words; nonsense:
优势	yōushì	(名) superiority; dominant position:
表面	biǎomiàn	(名) surface; face; outside; appearance:
手术	shǒushù	(名) surgical operation; operation:
系统	xìtǒng	(名) system:
制度	zhìdù	(名) system; institution:
太极拳	tàijí quán	(名) Taijiquan; Tai Chi; Shadowboxing
尾巴	wěibā	(名) tail
橘子	júzi	(名) tangerine
磁带	cídài	(名) tape (used in tape recorder)
目标	mùbiāo	(名) target; objective :

税	shuì	(名) tax; duty
教材	jiàocái	(名) teaching material
青少年	qīngshàonián	(名) teenagers:
寺庙	sìmiào	(名) temple; monastery
学期	xuéqí	(名) term; semester
恐怖	kǒngbù	(名) terror; horror
测验	cèyàn	(名) test
甲	jiǎ	(名) the first of the ten Heavenly Stems
心脏	xīnzàng	(名) the heart:
当代	Dāngdài	(名) the presen t age:
中旬	zhōngxún	(名) the second ten days of month
天空	tiānkōng	(名) the sky; the heaven
丝毫	sīháo	(名) the slightest amount or degree:
话题	huàtí	(名) theme of conversation
理论	lǐlùn	(名) theory
论文	lùnwén	(名) thesis; dissertation; treatise; paper:
事物	shìwù	(名) thing; object :
丙	bǐng	(名) third:

思想	sīxiǎng	(名) thought; thinking; idea; ideology :
嗓子	sǎngzi	(名) throat ; larynx:
雷	léi	(名) thunder
时刻	shíkè	(名) time; hour; moment:
期间	qíjiān	(名) time; period; course:
时代	shídài	(名) times; age; era; epoch:
罐头	guàntóu	(名) tin; can
题目	tímù	(名) title; subject; topic:
卫生间	wèishēngjiān	(名) toilet
声调	shēngdiào	(名) tone; note:
舌头	shétou	(名) tongue
顶	dǐng	(名) top; peak; summit:
傍晚	bàngwǎn	(名) toward evening; at nightfall; at dusk
塔	tǎ	(名) tower:
玩具	wánjù	(名) toy; plaything
贸易	màoyì	(名) trade:
行业	hángyè	(名) trade; profession; industry:
传统	chuántǒng	(名) tradition ; conventions:

电台	diàntái	(名) 1 radio station 2 transmitter receiver; transceiver
运输	yùnshū	(名) transport; carriage; conveyance:
宝贝	bǎobèi	(名) treasured object; treasure
趋势	qūshì	(名) trend; tendency:
实话	shíhuà	(名) truth:
真理	zhēnlǐ	(名) truth:
管子	guǎnzi	(名) tube; pipe
地道	dìdào	(名) tunnel
频道	píndào	(名) TV channel:
本科	běnkē	(名) undergraduate course; regular college course:
感受	gǎnshòu	(名) understanding; impression:
单位	dānwèi	(名) unit of an organization:
单元	dānyuán	(名) unit:
宇宙	yǔzhòu	(名) universe; cosmos.
用途	yòngtú	(名) use:
平常	píngcháng	(名) usually (形) ordinary; commonplace
蔬菜	shūcài	(名) vegetable

振动	zhèndòng	(名) vibration:
胜利	shènglì	(名) victory; triumph:
观点	guāndiǎn	(名) viewpoint; standpomt
醋	cù	(名) vinegar
病毒	bìngdú	(名) virus
业务	yèwù	(名) vocational work; professional work; business:
排球	páiqiú	(名) volleyball
册	cè	(名) volume;
体积	tǐjī	(名) volume; bulk
志愿者	zhìyuàn zhě	(名) volunteer:
腰	yāo	(名) waist
战争	zhànzhēng	(名) war: warfare:
方式	fāngshì	(名) way; fashion; pattern:
武器	wǔqì	(名) weapon; arms:
婚礼	hūnlǐ	(名) wedding ceremony; wedding
重量	zhòngliàng	(名) weight
小麦	xiǎomài	(名) wheat
整体	zhěngtǐ	(名) whole; (the situation) as a whole ; entirety:

翅膀	chìbǎng	(名) wing
狼	láng	(名) wolf
妇女	fùnǚ	(名) woman
工人	gōngrén	(名) worker; workman:
作品	zuòpǐn	(名) works (of literature and art)
烂	làn	(名) worn out (形) messy (动) rot; fester
毛笔	máo bǐ	(名) writing brush
非	fēi	(名) wrong; evildoing:
武术	wǔshù	(名) wushu , martial arts
青春	qīngchūn	(名) youth:
数码	shùmǎ	(名) 1 numeral 2 number; amount (形) digital
摩托车	mótuō chē	(名)motorcycle
智慧	zhìhuì	(名)wisdom; intelligence
木头	mùtou	(名)wood; log; timber

HSK 6 Nouns 名词 (918)

家   jiā   (名)[8] family

开水   kāishuǐ   (名) boiling water

屁股   pìgu   (名) buttocks; bottom:

界限   jièxiàn   (名) demarcation line; dividingline; limits; bounds; boundary

焦点   jiāodiǎn   (名) focal point; focus

夫人   fūrén   (名) Mrs. ; Madame; Lady:

气味   qìwèi   (名) smell; odour:

外界   wàijiè   (名) the external (or outside) world

轨道   guǐdào   (名) track

三角   sānjiǎo   (名) triangle

家伙   jiāhuo   (名) (口) fellow; guy

保姆   bǎomǔ   (名) (children's) nurse or domestic help

专科   zhuānkē   (名) (college for) professional training;

博览会   bólǎnhuì   (名) (international) fair; trade fair; expo (exposition, a show in which industrial goods, works of art, etc. are shown to the public)

---

[8](名) indicates 名词 míngcí Noun

战术	zhànshù	(名) (military) tactics:

原告   yuángào   (名) (of a civil case) plaintiff; (of a criminal case) prosecutor

出息   chūxī   (名) (of a person) promise; promising, shows signs that it is going to be successful

收益   shōuyì   (名) (of an enterprise) income; profit

副作用   fùzuòyòng   (名) (of medicine) side effect; by-effect

选手   xuǎnshǒu   (名) (of sports) selected contestant; player

财政   cáizhèng   (名) (public) finance:

嗅觉   xiùjué   (名) (sense of) smell:

阶层   jiēcéng   (名) (social) stratum:

处境   chǔjìng   (名) (usu.) unfavourable situation; plight:

水龙头   shuǐlóngtóu   (名) (water) tap; faucet; bibcock:

品质   pǐnzhí   (名) 1 (of a person) character; quality: 2 quality (of commodities. etc.):

情节   qíngjié   (名) 1 (of story, play, etc.) plot

2 circumstances:

当事人　　　dāngshìrén　　　(名) 1 (to a lawsuit) party; litigant; client

2 person concerned; interested party

修养　　　xiūyǎng　　　(名) 1 accomplishment; training 2 good manners

颗粒　　　kēlì　　　(名) 1 anything small and roundish (as a bean, pearl, etc.); pellet 2 grain:

附件　　　fùjiàn　　　(名) 1 appendix; annex 2 attachment, enclosure 3 (of a machine) accessory

武装　　　wǔzhuāng　　　(名) 1 arms; military equipment; battle outfit 2 armed forces 3 (动) equip (or supply) with arms; arm:

层次　　　céngcì　　　(名) 1 arrangement of ideas, colours etc. 2 administrative or education levels

反面　　　fǎnmiàn　　　(名) 1 back; reverse side; wrong side 2 negative side 3 opposite; the other side of the matter

旗帜　　　qízhì　　　(名) 1 banner; flag

依据　　　yījù　　　(名) 1 basis; foundation 2 (动) form a basis for action

阵容　　　zhènróng　　　(名) 1 battle array (or formation) 2 line-up

镜头　　　jìngtóu　　　(名) 1 camera lens: 2 shot; scene

| 卡通 | kǎtōng | (名) 1 caricature; cartoon 2 animated cartoon |

| 事业 | shìyè | (名) 1 cause; undertaking: 2 enterprise; facilities |

| 知觉 | zhījué | (名) 1 consciousness: 2 perception (the quality of |

being aware of things through the physical senses, especially sight)

| 角落 | jiǎoluò | (名) 1 corner 2 remote place: |

| 体面 | tǐmiàn | (名) 1 dignity; face 2 (形) honorable; creditable |

| 剧本 | jùběn | (名) 1 drama; play 2 script; (film) scenario; |

(Beijing opera, opera, etc.) libretto

| 端 | duān | (名) 1 end; extremely: |

| 产业 | chǎnyè | (名) 1 estate; property |

| 神气 | shénqì | (名) 1 expression; air; manner 2 putting on airs; |

cocky

| 眼光 | yǎnguāng | (名) 1 eye 2 sight; foresight; insight; vision |

| 出身 | chūshēn | (名) 1 family background 2 one's previous |

ocupation

| 心眼儿 | xīnyǎn er | (名) 1 heart; mind: 2 intelligence; cleverness: 3 |

unnecessary misgivings

| 高潮 | gāocháo | (名) 1 high tide 2 upsurge; climax: |

| 闲话 | xiánhuà | (名) 1 idle chat 2 complaint; gossip |

| 趣味 | qùwèi | (名) 1 interest; delight: 2 taste; liking: |

后代	hòudài	(名) 1 later periods (in history) 2 later generations; descendants
要点	yàodiǎn	(名) 1 main points; essentials, gist:
话筒	huàtǒng	(名) 1 microphone
模型	móxíng	(名) 1 model 2 mould; matrix; pattern
窝	wō	(名) 1 nest 2 lair; den
机构	jīgòu	(名) 1 organization; set-up 2 mechanism
疙瘩	gēda	(名) 1 pimple; lump; knot 2 misunderstanding; misgivings:
共鸣	gòngmíng	(名) 1 resonance 2 sympathetic response
现场	xiànchǎng	(名) 1 scene (of an accident or crime) 2 site; spot; (形) on-the-spot
潮流	cháoliú	(名) 1 tide 2 trend
时光	shíguāng	(名) 1 time 2 times; years; days
时代	shídài	(名) 1 times; age; era; epoch 2 a period in one's life:
口气	kǒuqì	(名) 1 tone; note 2 manner of speaking
队伍	duìwǔ	(名) 1 troops 2 procession; parade
口音	kǒuyīn	(名) 1 voice 2 accent (the way in which people in a particular area, country, or social group pronounce words)

哨	shào	(名) 1 whistle 2 sentry post; post:
事务	shìwù	(名) 1 work; routine 2 general affairs:
便条	biàntiáo	(名) a brief note
当务之急	dāngwùzhījí	(名) a burning issue of the moment; a top priority
栏目	lánmù	(名) a column (in a newspaper); a program (on TV)
课题	kètí	(名) a question for study or discussion
红包	hóngbāo	(名) a red paper envelope containing money as a gift; bonus
转折	zhuǎnzhé	(名) a turn in the course of events:
流氓	liúmáng	(名) a violent person who fights or causes damage or a person who behaving in ways that are not expected or not normal; rogue; hoodlum; hooligan; gangster
学历	xué lì	(名) a written account of one's education
本事	běnshì	(名) ability
才干	Cáigàn	(名) ability; competence
摘要	zhāiyào	(名) abstract; précis (a short form of a text that gives only the important parts)
弊端	bìduān	(名) abuse (the use of something in a way that is harmful or morally wrong); Corrupt practice (in public administration)
学位	xuéwèi	(名) academic degree:

事故	shì gù	(名) accident
伴随	bànsuí	(名) accompany ; follow
杂技	zájì	(名) acrobatics
司法	sīfǎ	(名) administration of justice; judicature (the legal system and the work it does)
行政	xíngzhèng	(名) administration:
利害	lìhài	(名) advantages and disadvantages; gains and losses: (形) terrible; formidable
顾问	gùwèn	(名) adviser; consultant
协议	xiéyì	(名) agreement:
酗酒	xùjiǔ	(名) alcoholism hit the bottle
终身	zhōngshēn	(名) all one's life:
常年	chángnián	(名) all the year round; for a very long period of time
联盟	liánméng	(名) alliance; league; coalition:
期限	qíxiàn	(名) allotted time; time limit; deadline:
沿海	yánhǎi	(名) along the coast; coastal
历来	lìlái	(名) always; all through the ages

州	zhōu	(名) an administrative division (state, prefecture, etc.)
片刻	piànkè	(名) an instant; a moment; a short while
变故	biàngù	(名) an unforeseen event; catastrophe (a bad situation)
比方	bǐfāng	(名) analogy ; instance :
麻醉	mázuì	(名) anesthesia; narcosis:
周年	zhōunián	(名) anniversary (the day on which an important event happened in a previous year)
公告	Gōnggào	(名) announcement; proclamation
对立	duìlì	(名) antagonism; antithesis; opposition:
古董	gǔdǒng	(名) antique:
对联	duìlián	(名) antithetical couplet (written on scrolls, etc.)
模样	múyàng	(名) appearance; look:
容貌	róngmào	(名) appearance; looks
胃口	wèikǒu	(名) appetite:
徒弟	túdì	(名) apprentice; disciple
区域	qūyù	(名) area; district; region
臂	bì	(名) arm

军队	jūnduì	(名) armed forces; army; troops
文艺	wényì	(名) art and literature
动脉	dòngmài	(名) artery
工艺品	gōngyìpǐn	(名) Arts & Crafts
局面	júmiàn	(名) aspect; phase; situation:
志气	zhìqì	(名) aspiration; ambition:
抱负	bàofù	(名) aspiration; ambition:
资产	zīchǎn	(名) assets; property; estate; capital:
助理	zhùlǐ	(名) assistant:
助手	zhùshǒu	(名) assistant; helper; aide
协会	xiéhuì	(名) association; society
天文	tiānwén	(名) astronomy:
起初	qǐchū	(名) at first; at the beginning
眼下	yǎnxià	(名) at the moment; at present; now:
气象	qìxiàng	(名) atmospheric phenomena:
气压	qìyā	(名) atmospheric pressure
乘务员	chéngwùyuán	(名) attendant on a train
伯母	bómǔ	(名) aunt; wife of father's eider brother

权威	quánwēi	(名) authority:
航空	hángkōng	(名) aviation:
娃娃	wáwá	(名) baby; child
婴儿	yīng'ér	(名) baby; infant
骨干	gǔgàn	(名) backbone; mainstay
备份	bèifèn	(名) back-up
丸	wán	(名) ball; pellet
钞票	chāopiào	(名) bank note
基地	jīdì	(名) base (the main place where a person lives and works, or a place that a company does business from)
盆地	péndì	(名) basin (the area of land from which streams run into a river, lake, or sea)
港湾	gǎngwān	(名) bay; harbour
床单	chuángdān	(名) bed sheet
凌晨	língchén	(名) before dawn
以往	yǐwǎng	(名) before; formerly; in the past:
先前	xiānqián	(名) before; previously:
乞丐	qǐgài	(名) beggar
效益	xiàoyì	(名) beneficial result; benefit :

仁慈	réncí	(名) benevolence; mercy
都市	dūshì	(名) big city; metropolis
传记	zhuànjì	(名) biography
飞禽走兽	fēiqín zǒushòu	(名) birds and beasts; fauna
诞辰	dànchén	(名) birthday
屑	xiè	(名) bits; scrapes; crumbs:
空白	kòngbái	(名) blank space
血压	xiěyā	(名) blood pressure:
舟	zhōu	(名) boat:
债券	zhàiquàn	(名) bond:
书籍	shūjí	(名) books; works
边境	biānjìng	(名) border ; frontier:
边疆	biānjiāng	(名) border; borderland; frontier; frontier region
边界	biānjiè	(名) boundary; border:
弦	xián	(名) bowstring; string
岔	chà	(名) branch; fork (road) (动) branch off :
缺口	quēkǒu	(名) breach; gap:
贿赂	huìlù	(名) bribe

砖瓦	zhuān wǎ	(名) brick and tile
新娘	xīnniáng	(名) bride (a woman who is about to get married or has just got married)
新郎	xīnláng	(名) bridegroom (a man who is about to get married or has just got married)
桥梁	qiáoliáng	(名) bridge
锦绣前程	jǐnxiù qiánchéng	(名) bright future
棕色	zōngsè	(名) brown
预算	yùsuàn	(名) budget:
子弹	zǐdàn	(名) bullet
丰收	fēngshōu	(名) bumper harvest:
负担	fùdān	(名) burden; load:
交易	jiāoyì	(名) business; deal; trade; transaction:
纽扣儿	niǔ kòu er	(名) button (of cloth)
舱	cāng	(名) cabin:
运算	yùnsuàn	(名) calculation; operation
号召	hàozhào	(名) call; appeal (a request to the public for money, information, or help)
战役	zhànyì	(名) campaign; battle

癌症	áizhèng	(名) cancer
候选	hòuxuǎn	(名) candidate :
糖葫芦	tánghúlu	(名) Candied fruit; candied haws on a stick
本钱	běnqián	(名) capital (money)
资本	zīběn	(名) capital:
二氧化碳	èryǎnghuàtàn	(名) Carbon dioxide
疏忽	shūhū	(名) carelessness; negligence; oversight
漫画	mànhuà	(名) caricature; cartoon
城堡	chéngbǎo	(名) castle
灾难	zāinàn	(名) catastrophe; suffering; disaster; calamity
范畴	fànchóu	(名) category, categories, scope
洞穴	dòngxué	(名) cave; cavern (a large cave)
细胞	xìbāo	(名) cell
摄氏度	shèshìdù	(名) Celsius
水泥	shuǐní	(名) cement
中央	zhōngyāng	(名) center; middle:
典礼	diǎnlǐ	(名) ceremony; celebration
仪式	yíshì	(名) ceremony; rite:

证书	zhèngshū	(名) certificate; credentials:
颈椎	jǐngchuí	(名) cervical vertebra
连锁	liánsuǒ	(名) Chain; Chains; Interlock
董事长	dǒngshì zhǎng	(名) chairman of the board

变迁　biànqiān　(名) changes; vicissitudes (changes that happen at different times during the life or development of someone or something, especially those that result in conditions being worse)

特色	tèsè	(名) characteristic; distinguishing feature (or quality)
腮	sāi	(名) cheek
化验	huàyàn	(名) chemical examination; laboratory test:
化肥	huàféi	(名) chemical fertilizer
旗袍	qípáo	(名) Cheongsam; a Traditional Chinese woman dress
胸膛	xiōngtáng	(名) chest

重阳节　chóngyáng jié　(名) chongyang festival; the double ninth festival

公民	gōngmín	(名) citizen:
条款	tiáokuǎn	(名) clause; article; provision:
悬崖峭壁	xuányá qiàobì	(名) Cliffs
衣裳	yīshang	(名) clothing; clothes

包袱	bāofú	(名) cloth-wrapper 3 load; weight; burden:
棍棒	gùnbàng	(名) club; cudgel; stick
线索	xiànsuǒ	(名) clue
高考	gāokǎo	(名) college entrance examination (gaokao, the highly competitive college entrance exam that decides the fortunes of so many young Chinese people.)
殖民地	zhímíndì	(名) colony
色彩	sècǎi	(名) colour; hue; tint; shade:
司令	sīlìng	(名) commander; commanding officer:
委员	wěiyuán	(名) committee member :
俗话	súhuà	(名) common saying; proverb:
社区	shèqū	(名) community
伴侣	bànlǚ	(名) companion; mate; partner:
指南针	zhǐnánzhēn	(名) compass
抱怨	bàoyuàn	(名) complain; grumble
落成	luòchéng	(名) completion (of a building. etc.):
气色	qìsè	(名) complexion; colour:
同志	tóngzhì	(名) comrade (a member of the same political group, especially a communist or socialist group or a trade union)

调料	tiáoliào	(名) condiment; seasoning; flavouring
地步	dìbù	(名) condition ; situation; plight (an unpleasant condition, especially a serious, sad, or difficult one)
情形	qíngxíng	(名) condition; situation;
品行	pǐnxíng	(名) conduct; behaviour:
混乱	hǔnluàn	(名) confusion; chaos:
内涵	nèihán	(名) connotation
良心	liángxīn	(名) conscience:
宪法	xiànfǎ	(名) constitution
领事馆	lǐngshìguǎn	(名) consulate (the office where a consul works)
用户	yònghù	(名) consumer; user:
竞赛	jìngsài	(名) contest; competition; emulation; race:
争端	zhēngduān	(名) controversial issue; dispute; conflict :
烹饪	pēngrèn	(名) cooking; culinary art:
铜矿	tóng kuàng	(名) copper mine; copper ore
重心	zhòngxīn	(名) core; focus 2 centre of gravity
尸体	shītǐ	(名) corpse; dead body; remains:
走廊	zǒuláng	(名) corridor: passage

贪污	tānwū	(名) corruption; graft:
成本	chéngběn	(名) cost:
对策	duìcè	(名) countermeasure
礼节	lǐjié	(名) courtesy; etiquette; protocol; ceremony:
手艺	shǒuyì	(名) craftsmanship; workmanship
精华	jīnghuá	(名) cream; essence; quintessence
功劳	gōngláo	(名) credit; contribution (to a cause)
刑事	xíngshì	(名) criminal; penal:
危机	wéijī	(名) crisis:
文物	wénwù	(名) cultural relics; historical relics
时事	shíshì	(名) current affairs
习俗	xísú	(名) custom; convention
客户	kèhù	(名) customer
舞蹈	wǔdǎo	(名) dance; dancing
魄力	pòlì	(名) daring and resolution; boldness:
气魄	qìpò	(名) daring; boldness of vision; imposing manner
黎明	límíng	(名) dawn; daybreak
清晨	qīngchén	(名) dawn; early morning.

昼夜	zhòuyè	(名) day and night; round the clock
演绎	yǎnyì	(名) deduction:
事迹	shìjì	(名) deed; achievement :
缺陷	quēxiàn	(名) defect; drawback; flaw
防御	fángyù	(名) defence
被告	bèigào	(名) defendant; the accused
赤字	chìzì	(名) deficit
定义	dìngyì	(名) definition:
佳肴	jiāyáo	(名) delicacies
乐趣	lèqù	(名) delight; pleasure; joy :
论证	lùnzhèng	(名) demonstration; proof
密度	mìdù	(名) density; thickness:
押金	yājīn	(名) deposit; security
贬义	biǎnyì	(名) derogatory sense :
欲望	yùwàng	(名) desire; wish ; lust (a very powerful feeling of wanting something)
侦探	zhēntàn	(名) detective
偏差	piānchā	(名) deviation; error

魔鬼	móguǐ	(名) devil; demon; monster
方言	fāngyán	(名) dialect
钻石	zuànshí	(名) diamond
腹泻	fùxiè	(名) diarrhoea
独裁	dúcái	(名) dictatorship; autocratic rule:
柴油	cháiyóu	(名) diesel oil:
尊严	zūnyán	(名) dignity; honour:
文凭	wénpíng	(名) diploma
处分	chǔfèn	(名) disciplinary action; punishment:
牢骚	láosāo	(名) discontent; grievance; complaint:
疾病	jíbìng	(名) disease; illness:
部署	bùshǔ	(名) dispose; deploy; make arrangements for sth.
争议	zhēngyì	(名) dispute; controversy:
分歧	fēnqí	(名) dispute; difference; divergence:
纠纷	jiūfēn	(名) dispute; issue:
风味	fēngwèi	(名) distinctive flavour; local colour:
多元化	duōyuán huà	(名) Diversification; Pluralism
文献	wénxiàn	(名) document; literature:

犬	quǎn	(名) dog (more formal than 狗）
家常	jiācháng	(名) domestic trivia
羽绒服	yǔróngfú	(名) down jacket; down and feather garment
草案	cǎo'àn	(名) draft (of a plan, law, etc.):
弊病	bìbìng	(名) drawback ; disadvantage
渣	zhā	(名) dregs; sediment; residue
毒品	dúpǐn	(名) Drug; narcotics
黄昏	huánghūn	(名) dusk, the time before night when it is not yet dark
堤坝	dībà	(名) dykes and dam.
耳环	ěrhuán	(名) earings
生态	shēngtài	(名) ecology (the relationships between the air, land, water, animals, plants, etc., usually of a particular area, or the scientific study of this)
边缘	biānyuán	(名) edge; fringe; verge; brink
成效	chéngxiào	(名) effect; result:
功效	gōngxiào	(名) efficacy; effect
弹性	tánxìng	(名) elasticity; resilience; spring (something's ability to return to its usual shape after it has been pressed)

| 嫂子 | sǎozi | (名) elder brother sister-in-law |

长辈　　　　zhǎngbèi　　　　(名) elder member of a family; one's senior

电源　　　　diànyuán　　　　(名) electric power supply; mains (a large pipe that carries water or gas, or a wire carrying electricity, from one place to another, to which a house can be connected)

风度　　　　fēngdù　　　　(名) elegant manners:

元素　　　　yuánsù　　　　(名) element

椭圆　　　　tuǒyuán　　　　(名) ellipse; oval

泰斗　　　　tàidǒu　　　　(名) Eminent scholar;

终点　　　　zhōngdiǎn　　　　(名) end point ; destination:

能量　　　　néngliàng　　　　(名) energy

引擎　　　　yǐnqíng　　　　(名) engine

启示　　　　qǐshì　　　　(名) enlightening guidance; illuminating remarks

防疫　　　　fángyì　　　　(名) epidemic prevention:

器材　　　　qìcái　　　　(名) equipment; material:

误差　　　　wùchā　　　　(名) error :

要素　　　　yàosù　　　　(名) essential factor

隔阂　　　　géhé　　　　(名) estrangement; misunderstanding:

酒精　　　　jiǔjīng　　　　(名) ethyl alcohol; alcohol

欧洲	ōuzhōu	(名) Europe:
进化	jìnhuà	(名) evolution:
例外	lìwài	(名) exception:
注释	zhùshì	(名) explanatory note; annotation
曝光	pùguāng	(名) exposure
眼神	yǎnshén, yǎnshen	(名) expression in one's eyes; meaningful glance; wink:
神态	shéntài	(名) expression; carnage; bearing
神情	shénqíng	(名) expression; look
神色	shénsè	(名) expression; look
境界	jìngjiè	(名) extent reached; plane attained; state; realm:
外表	wàibiǎo	(名) exterior; surface
外向	wàixiàng	(名) Extrovert (an energetic happy person who enjoys being with other people); open character
寓言	yùyán	(名) fable; allegory; parable
面貌	miànmào	(名) face; features
童话	tónghuà	(名) fairy tales
信念	xìnniàn	(名) faith; belief; conviction
名誉	míngyù	(名) fame; reputation:

天伦之乐	tiānlún zhī lè	(名) family happiness; domestic felicity
家属	jiāshǔ	(名) family members; (family) dependents
时装	shízhuāng	(名) fashionable dress; the latest fashion:
脂肪	zhīfáng	(名) fat:
过失	guòshī	(名) fault; error; slip
失误	shīwù	(名) fault; mistake
反馈	fǎnkuì	(名) feedback
恩怨	ēnyuàn	(名) feelings of gratitude or resentment:
纤维	xiānwéi	(名) fibre:
视野	shìyě	(名) field of vision
档案	dǎng'àn	(名) files; archives; record:
馅儿	xiàn er	(名) filling; stuffing
结局	jiéjú	(名) final result; outcome; ending:
财务	cáiwù	(名) financial affairs
消防	xiāofáng	(名) fire control; fire fighting:
烟花爆竹	yānhuā bàozhú	(名) Fireworks and firecrackers
渔民	yúmín	(名) fisherman
拳头	quántóu	(名) fist

火焰	huǒyàn	(名) flame
洪水	hóngshuǐ	(名) flood; flood water
荧屏	yíngpíng	(名) fluorescent screen
泡沫	pàomò	(名) foam; froth
饮食	yǐnshí	(名) food and drink:
势力	shìlì	(名) force ; power; influence :
格式	géshì	(名) form; pattern:
公式	gōngshì	(名) formula; equation
论坛	lùntán	(名) forum; tribune
化石	huà shí	(名) fossil
框架	kuàngjià	(名) frame
频率	pínlǜ	(名) frequency
淡水	dànshuǐ	(名) fresh water
浑身	húnshēn	(名) from head to foot; all over:
同胞兄弟	tóngbāo xiōngdì	(名) full brothers; 2 fellow countryman; compatriot

(a person who comes from the same country)

| 性能 | xìngnéng | (名) function (of a machine, etc.); property; |

performance

| 职能 | zhínéng | (名) function: |

基金	jījīn	(名) fund (an amount of money saved, collected, or provided for a particular purpose)
经费	jīngfèi	(名) funds; outlay; expenditure; expenses
赌博	dǔbó	(名) gambling
匪徒	fěitú	(名) gangster; bandit
差距	chājù	(名) gap; disparity; difference :
基因	jīyīn	(名) gene
将军	jiāngjūn	(名) general (an officer of very high rank, especially in the army)
大意	dàyi	(名) general idea; main points; gist 2 (形) careless
风气	fēngqì	(名) general mood; common practice; atmosphere:
天才	tiāncái	(名) genius; talent; gift; endowment:
绅士	shēnshì	(名) gentleman; gentry
地质	dìzhí	(名) geology
细菌	xìjùn	(名) germs; bacteria
手势	shǒushì	(名) gesture; sign; signal
榜样	bǎngyàng	(名) good example ; model
机遇	jīyù	(名) good fortune; opportunity
物资	wùzī	(名) goods and materials:

次品	cì pǐn	(名) goods of poor quality; defective goods
峡谷	xiágǔ	(名) gorge; canyon
档次	dàngcì	(名) Grade; level
等级	děngjí	(名) grade; rank
祖父	zǔfù	(名) grandfather
坟墓	fénmù	(名) grave; tomb
气势	qìshì	(名) great force of imposing posture:
深情厚谊	shēnqíng hòuyì	(名) great kindness and cordiality
盛情	shèngqíng	(名) great kindness; boundless hospitality:
集团	jítuán	(名) group; clique; circle; bloc:
派别	pàibié	(名) group; school; faction
发育	fāyù	(名) growth (the growth of a person, animal, or plant is its process of increasing in size.); development:
粥	zhōu	(名) gruel; porridge
导弹	dǎodàn	(名) guided missile
方针	fāngzhēn	(名) guiding principle; policy
纲领	gānglǐng	(名) guiding principle; programme
火药	huǒyào	(名) gunpowder

往常	wǎngcháng	(名) habitually in the past:
冰雹	bīngbáo	(名) hail
锤	chuí	(名) hammer
把手	bǎshǒu	(名) handle; grip; knob
福气	fúqi	(名) happy lot; good fortune; be blessed
元首	yuánshǒu	(名) head of state; monarch
正气	zhèngqì	(名) healthy trends (or tendencies)
海拔	hǎibá	(名) height above sea level; elevation:
遗传	yíchuán	(名) heredity; inheritance:
隐患	yǐnhuàn	(名) hidden trouble; hidden danger; snake in the grass:
上级	shàngjí	(名) higher level; higher authorities:
丘陵	qiūlíng	(名) hills:
孔	kǒng	(名) hole; opening; aperture:
坑	kēng	(名) hole; pit; hollow:
钩子	gōuzi	(名) hook
东道主	dōngdàozhǔ	(名) host
人质	rénzhì	(名) hostage

人性	rénxìng	(名) human nature; humanity
人道	réndào	(名) humanity; human sympathy
风趣	fēngqù	(名) humour; wit:
夫妇	fūfù	(名) husband and wife:
公婆	gōngpó	(名) husband's father and mother
氢	qīng	(名) hydrogen (H):
空想	kōngxiǎng	(名) idle dream; fantasy; utopia
免疫	miǎnyì	(名) immunity (from disease)
声势	shēngshì	(名) impetuous force:
昔日	xīrì	(名) in former times
跟前	gēnqián	(名) in front of; near:
热门	rèmén	(名) in great demand; popular
连年	liánnián	(名) in successive or consecutive years; for years running
事件	shìjiàn	(名) incident; event
个体	gètǐ	(名) individual:
推理	tuīlǐ	(名) inference ; reasoning:
推论	tuīlùn	(名) inference; deduction; corollary (something that results from something else.

通货膨胀	tōnghuò péngzhàng	(名) inflation.
情报	qíngbào	(名) inforrnation; intelligence:
墨水儿	mòshuǐ er	(名) ink
昆虫	kūnchóng	(名) insect
内幕	nèimù	(名) Inside story; what goes on behind the scenes
灵感	línggǎn	(名) inspiration
本能	běnnéng	(名) instinct
仪器	yíqì	(名) instrument; apparatus:
智商	zhìshāng	(名) intelligence quotient; IQ
智力	zhìlì	(名) intelligence; intellect:
意图	yìtú	(名) intention; intent
意向	yìxiàng	(名) intention; purpose
互联网	hùliánwǎng	(名) internet
空隙	kòngxì	(名) interspace; spacing; interstice
请帖	qǐng tiě	(名) invitation
请柬	qǐngjiǎn	(名) invitation card
渠道	qúdào	(名) irrigation ditch 2 medium of communication; channel

水利	shuǐlì	(名) irrigation works; water conservancy project:
岛屿	dǎoyǔ	(名) islands
事项	shìxiàng	(名) item; matter:
本身	běnshēn	(名) itself:
罐	guàn	(名) Jar : canister; tin:
碧玉	bìyù	(名) jasper (an opaque reddish-brown variety of chalcedony), green jade.
裁判	cáipàn	(名) judgment; referee
丛林	cónglín	(名) jungle; forest
正义	zhèngyì	(名) justice (形) just; righteous
公道	gōngdào	(名) justice:
炉灶	lúzào	(名) kitchen range; cooking range:
膝盖	xīgài	(名) knee
湖泊	húbó	(名) lakes
园林	yuánlín	(名) landscape garden
巷	xiàng	(名) lane; alley
灯笼	dēnglóng	(名) lantern
大厦	dàshà	(名) large building

潜力	qiánlì	(名) latent capacity; potential; potentiality:
经纬	jīngwěi	(名) latitude and longitude
案件	ànjiàn	(名) law case; case:
案例	ànlì	(名) law case; case:
诉讼	sùsòng	(名) lawsuit
外行	wàiháng	(名) layman; nonprofessional
领袖	lǐngxiù	(名) leader
传单	chuándān	(名) leaflet; handbill
皮革	pígé	(名) leather and fur
遗产	yíchǎn	(名) legacy ; inheritance:
法人	fǎrén	(名) legal person
字母	zìmǔ	(名) letters (of an alphabet):
杠杆	gànggǎn	(名) lever
性命	xìngmìng	(名) life (the period between birth and death, or the experience or state of being alive)
视线	shìxiàn	(名) line of sight; sight; attention
环节	huánjié	(名) link: 2 segment
嘴唇	zuǐchún	(名) lip

牲畜	shēngchù	(名) livestock; domestic animals
生物	shēngwù	(名) living things; living beings; organisms; biology (short form for 生物学)
风土人情	fēngtǔ rénqíng	(名) local conditions and customs
气概	qìgài	(名) lofty; spirit
亏损	kuīsǔn	(名) loss; deficit:
彩票	cǎipiào	(名) lottery ticket
喇叭	lǎbā	(名) loudspeaker; honk
机械	jīxiè	(名) machinery; machine; mechanism:
魔术	móshù	(名) magic; conjuring
壮观	zhuàngguān	(名) magnificent sight
主流	zhǔliú	(名) main stream 2 essential aspect; main trend
宏旨	hóngzhǐ	(名) main theme; cardinal principle:
雌雄	cíxióng	(名) male and female:
稿件	gǎojiàn	(名) manuscript; contribution
痕迹	hénjī	(名) mark; trace; vestige (a small part or amount of something larger, stronger, or more important that still exists from something that existed in the past)
沼泽	zhǎozé	(名) marsh; swamp

含义	hányì	(名) meaning; implication:
媒体	méitǐ	(名) media
媒介	méijiè	(名) medium; vehicle:
旋律	xuánlǜ	(名) melody
成员	chéngyuán	(名) member:
膜	mó	(名) membrane:
备忘录	bèiwànglù	(名) memorandum; aide-memoire
记性	jìxìng	(名) memory:
心态	xīntài	(名) Mentality; Attitude; Mind
新陈代谢	xīnchéndàixiè	(名) metabolism
比喻	bǐyù	(名) metaphor; analogy; figure of speech:
里程碑	lǐchéngbēi	(名) milestone:
毫米	háomǐ	(名) millimetre.
胸怀	xiōnghuái	(名) mind; heart:
大臣	dàchén	(名) minister (of a monarchy)
使命	shǐmìng	(名) mission:
模范	mófàn	(名) model; fine example (to follow)
模式	móshì	(名) model; mode; pattern; type

造型	zàoxíng	(名) model; mould:
压岁钱 gift	yāsuìqián	(名) money glven to children as a lunar New Year
货币	huòbì	(名) money; currency:
品德	pǐndé	(名) moral character
霞	xiá	(名) morning or evening glow:
母语	mǔyǔ	(名) mother tongue
动机	dòngjī	(名) motive; intention:
座右铭	zuòyòumíng	(名) motto (a short sentence or phrase that expresses a belief or purpose)
山脉	shānmài	(名) mountam range; mountain chain
举动	jǔdòng	(名) move; act; conduct
凶手	xiōngshǒu	(名) murderer; assassin
乐谱	yuèpǔ	(名) music score
节奏	jiézòu	(名) musical rhythm:
近视	jìnshì	(名) myopia; nearsightedness; shortsightedness
指甲	zhǐjiǎ	(名) nail:
齐心协力	qíxīn xiélì	(名) nasal mucus (a thick liquid produced inside the nose) ; snot (mucus produced in the nose)

鼻涕　　　　bítì　　　　　　　（名）nasal mucus (a thick liquid produced inside

the nose); snivel:

国防　　　　guófáng　　　　　（名）national defence

故乡　　　　gùxiāng　　　　　（名）native place; hometown

天然气　　　tiānránqì　　　　　（名）natural gas

自然　　　　zìrán　　　　　　　（名）nature:

舰艇　　　　jiàntǐng　　　　　　（名）naval ships and boats; naval vessels

导航　　　　dǎoháng　　　　　（名）navigation

网络　　　　wǎngluò　　　　　（名）network; The internet

报社　　　　bàoshè　　　　　　（名）newspaper office

贵族　　　　guìzú　　　　　　　（名）noble; aristocrat; aristocracy

噪音　　　　zàoyīn　　　　　　（名）noise

准则　　　　zhǔnzé　　　　　　（名）norm; standard; criterion:

公证　　　　gōngzhèng　　　　（名）notarization:

启事　　　　qǐshì　　　　　　　（名）notice; announcement

布告　　　　bùgào　　　　　　（名）notice; bulletin; proclamation:

数目　　　　shùmù　　　　　　（名）number; amount

数额	shù'é	(名) number; amount
数	shù	(名) number; figure [数 shǔ (动) to count]
桨	jiǎng	(名) oar (a long pole with a wide, flat part at one end, used for rowing a boat)
障碍	zhàng'ài	(名) obstacle; impediment:
场合	chǎnghé	(名) occasion (a special or formal event)
机关	jīguān	(名) office; organ; body (of goverment)
公务	gōngwù	(名) official duty:
淡季	dànjì	(名) off-season
预兆	yùzhào	(名) omen; sign; harbinger (a person or thing that shows that something is going to happen soon, especially something bad)
本人	běnrén	(名) oneself; in person:
言论	yánlùn	(名) opinion on politics and other affairs
时机	shíjī	(名) opportunity; an opportune moment:
口腔	kǒuqiāng	(名) oral cavity:
橙	chéng	(名) orange; orange color
指令	zhǐlìng	(名) order; instruction:
次序	cìxù	(名) order; sequence
团体	tuántǐ	(名) orgamzation; group; team:

来历	láilì	(名) origin; source; antecedents; background; past history:
当初	dāngchū	(名) originally; in the beginning; in the first place:
太空	tàikōng	(名) outer space.
轮廓	lúnkuò	(名) outline; contour; rough sketch
门诊	ménzhěn	(名) outpatient service (in a hospital):
布局	bùjú	(名) overall arrangement; layout; distribution:
全局	quánjú	(名) overall situation:
立交桥	lìjiāoqiáo	(名) overpass; flyover; motorway interchange
华侨	huáqiáo	(名) overseas Chinese
氧气	yǎngqì	(名) oxygen
稻谷	dàogǔ	(名) paddy; (unhusked) rice; rice in the husk; grains
心血	xīnxuè	(名) painstaking effort:
油漆	yóuqī	(名) paint (a coloured liquid that is put on a surface such as a wall to decorate it) (动) cover with paint; to paint
宫殿	gōngdiàn	(名) palace
天堂	Tiāntáng	(名) paradise; heaven:

麻痹	mábì	(名) paralysis (动) benumb; lull: (形) lacking in vigilance:
局部	júbù	(名) part (as opposed to the whole):
片段	piànduàn	(名) part ; passage; fragment:
搭档`	dādàng `	(名) partner
历代	lìdài	(名) past dynasties
往事	wǎngshì	(名) past events
专利	zhuānlì	(名) patent:
患者	huànzhě	(名) patient ; sufferer
图案	tú'àn	(名) pattern; design
格局	géjú	(名) pattern; set-up; structure；format, situation
款式	kuǎnshì	(名) pattern; style; design
高峰	gāofēng	(名) peak; summit; height:
珍珠	zhēnzhū	(名) pearl
书法	shūfǎ	(名) penmanship; calligraphy
周期	zhōuqí	(名) period; cycle
人士	rénshì	(名) personage; public figure:
人格	réngé	(名) personality; character; moral quality:

花瓣	huābàn	(名) petal (of flower)
石油	shíyóu	(名) petroleum; oil
地势	dì shì	(名) physical features of a place; relief
器官	qìguān	(名) physical organ:
生理	shēnglǐ	(名) physiology; (the scientific study of) the way

in which the bodies of living things work

支柱	zhīzhù	(名) pillar; prop; mainstay
粉色	fěnsè	(名) pink colour
场所	chǎngsuǒ	(名) place (for certain activities)
平原	píngyuán	(名) plain; flat lands
辫子	biànzi	(名) plait; braid; pigtail:
规划	guīhuà	(名) plan; programme; Programming, Planning
平面	píngmiàn	(名) plane (in mathematics, a flat or level surface

that continues in all directions)

阴谋	yīnmóu	(名) plot; scheme; conspiracy:
党	dǎng	(名) political party:
政权	zhèngquán	(名) political power [compare with （政府

zhèngfǔ government (the group of people who officially control a country)]

池塘	chítáng	(名) pond; pool

港口	gǎngkǒu	(名) port; harbour
肖像	xiàoxiàng	(名) portrait; portraiture .
阵地	zhèndì	(名) position ; front :
名次	míngcì	(名) position in a name list; place in a competition:
部位	bùwèi	(名) position; place; location
职位	zhíwèi	(名) position; post
立场	lìchǎng	(名) position; stand; standpoint:
正负	zhèng fù	(名) Positive and negative (in electronic)
岗位	gǎngwèi	(名) post:
职务	zhíwù	(名) post; duty
姿态	zītài	(名) posture; gesture
陶瓷	táocí	(名) pottery and porcelain; ceramics
磅	bàng	(名) pound (动) to weigh
粉末	fěnmò	(名) Powder
动力	dònglì	(名) power 2 driving force; motivation; impetus
威力	wēilì	(名) power; might
序言	xùyán	(名) preface; foreword
偏见	piānjiàn	(名) prejudice; bias:

预赛　　　　yùsài　　　　　　　（名）preliminaries (an event or action that introduces or prepares for something else)

前提　　　　qiántí　　　　　　　（名）premise; prerequisite; precondition

现状　　　　xiànzhuàng　　　　　（名）present situation; existing state of affairs; status quo

当前　　　　dāngqián　　　　　　（名）present; current:

威望　　　　wēiwàng　　　　　　（名）prestige

信誉　　　　xìnyù　　　　　　　（名）prestige; credit; reputation:

威信　　　　wēixìn　　　　　　　（名）prestige; popular trust

代价　　　　dàijià　　　　　　　（名）price; cost:

原理　　　　yuánlǐ　　　　　　　（名）principle a basic idea or rule that explains or controls how something happens or works

监狱　　　　jiānyù　　　　　　　（名）prison; jail

隐私　　　　yǐnsī　　　　　　　（名）private matters one wants to hush up or refrains from talking about:

加工　　　　jiāgōng　　　　　　（名）process (a method of producing goods in a factory by treating natural substances) 2 machining; working

盈利　　　　yínglì　　　　　　　（名）profit; gain

奥秘　　　　àomì　　　　　　　（名）profound mystery

条理	tiáolǐ	(名) proper arrangement or presentation; orderliness; method:
比重	bǐzhòng	(名) proportion:
散文	sǎnwén	(名) prose; essay
前景	qiánjǐng	(名) prospect; perspective:
屏障	píngzhàng	(名) protective screen:
蛋白质	dànbáizhí	(名) protein
省会	shěnghuì	(名) provincial capital
舆论	yúlùn	(名) public opinion
治安	zhì'ān	(名) public order or security:
公关	gōngguān	(名) Public Relations; PR
公安局	gōng'ān jú	(名) public security bureau. ; police station
刊物	kānwù	(名) publication:
脉搏	màibó	(名) pulse
气功	qìgōng	(名) qigong , a system of deep breathing exercises
素质	sùzhì	(名) quality; performance; capability
季度	jìdù	(名) quarter (of a year):
种族	zhǒngzú	(名) race (a group, especially of people)

雷达	léidá	(名) radar
光辉	guānghuī	(名) radiance; brilliance; glory:
辐射	fúshè	(名) radiation
收音机	shōuyīnjī	(名) radio (set); wireless (set):
幅度	fúdù	(名) range: scope: extent:
级别	jíbié	(名) rank; level; grade; scale:
行列	hángliè	(名) ranks:
利率	lìlù	(名) rate of interest; interest rate
光芒	guāngmáng	(名) rays of light; radiance
实惠	shíhuì	(名) real benefit; (形) practical; have real benefit
后勤	hòuqín	(名) rear service; logistics:
理智	lǐzhì	(名) reason; intellect:
情理	qínglǐ	(名) reason; sense
近来	Jìnlái	(名) recently; of late; lately
反思	fǎnsī	(名) Reflections on （serious and careful thought on sth)
报答	bàodá	(名) repay; requite:
共和国	gònghéguó	(名) republic

面子	miànzi	(名) reputation; face; self-respect:
声誉	shēngyù	(名) reputation; fame; prestige
需求	xūqiú	(名) requirement; demand
住宅	zhùzhái	(名) residence

残留　cánliú　(名) residue (the part that is left after the main part has gone or been taken away, or a substance that remains after a chemical process such as evaporation)

报酬	bàochóu	(名) reward; remuneration; pay:

是非　shìfēi　(名) right and wrong; truth and falsehood 2 quarrel; dispute

权益	quányì	(名) rights and interests:
岩石	yánshí	(名) rock
火箭	huǒjiàn	(名) rocket

歹徒　dǎitú　(名) ruffian (a violent, wild, and unpleasant person, usually a man); evildoer

废墟	fèixū	(名) ruins
规章	guīzhāng	(名) rule; regulation:
章程	zhāngchéng	(名) rules; constitution
谣言	yáoyán	(名) rumour:

薪水	xīnshuǐ	(名) salary; pay
唾沫	tuòmò	(名) saliva; spittle
样品	yàngpǐn	(名) sample (product); specimen
卫星	wèixīng	(名) satellite
饱和	bǎohé	(名) saturation (to reach a stage where no more can be added, contained, or accepted)
疤	bā	(名) scar
场面	chǎngmiàn	(名) scene (in drama, fiction, etc.); event; occasion
风光	Fēngguāng	(名) scene; view; sight:
功课	gōngkè	(名) schoolwork; homework
螺丝钉	luósīdīng	(名) screw
雕塑	diāosù	(名) sculpture
海滨	hǎibīn	(名) seashore; seaside:
亚军	yàjūn	(名) second place (in a sports contest)
书记	shūjì	(名) secretary:
种子	zhǒngzǐ	(名) seed
检讨	jiǎntǎo	(名) self-criticism
分寸	fēncùn	(名) sense of propriety:

羞耻	xiūchǐ	(名) sense of shame; shame:
系列	xìliè	(名) set; series:
挫折	cuòzhé	(名) setback; reverse:
严寒	yánhán	(名) severe cold; bitter cold
形态	xíngtài	(名) shape; morphology (the scientific study of the structure and form of animals and plants)
股份	gǔfèn	(名) share; stock
股东	gǔdōng	(名) shareholder; stock holder
贝壳	bèiké	(名) shell
船舶	chuánbó	(名) ship.
畔	pàn	(名) side; bank
侧面	cèmiàn	(名) side; profile:
目光	mùguāng	(名) sight; vision; view:
迹象	jīxiàng	(名) sign; indica tion :
标记	biāojì	(名) sign; mark; symbol
简体字	jiǎntǐzì	(名) Simplified characters; Simplified Chinese characters
局势	júshì	(名) situation:
手法	shǒufǎ	(名) skill; technique 2 trick; gimmick

奴隶	núlì	(名) slave
坡	pō	(名) slope:
溪	xī	(名) small stream; brook
土壤	tǔrǎng	(名) soil
曲子	qǔzi	(名) song; tune; melody
媳妇	xífù	(名) son's wife; daughter-in-law
灵魂	línghún	(名) soul; spirit
动静	dòngjìng	(名) sound of people speaking or moving about:
音响	yīnxiǎng	(名) sound; acoustics:
源泉	yuánquán	(名) source; fountainhead:
来源	láiyuán	(名) source; origin:
根源	gēnyuán	(名) source; origin; root:
主权	zhǔquán	(名) sovereign rights; sovereignty:
航天	hángtiān	(名) spaceflight:
专长	zhuāncháng	(名) special skill or knowledge; specialty:
特长	tècháng	(名) special skill; special work experience
专题	zhuāntí	(名) special subject (or topic)
规格	guīgé	(名) specifications; standards:

标本	biāoběn	(名) specimen; sample:
纺织	fǎngzhī	(名) spinning and weaving:
光彩	guāngcǎi	(名) splendor; brilliance; radiance:
配偶	pèi'ǒu	(名) spouse
间谍	jiàndié	(名) spy
规范	guīfàn	(名) standard; norm:
事态	shìtài	(名) state of affairs; situation:
轮船	lún chuán	(名) steamer; steamship; steamboat
秤	chèng	(名) steelyard; scale
步伐	bùfá	(名) step; pace:
茎	jīng	(名) stern (of a plant); stalk

战略 zhànlüè (名) strategy (a detailed plan for achieving success in situations such as war, politics, business, industry, or sport, or the skill of planning for such situations)

实力 shílì (名) strength (the ability to do things that need a lot of physical or mental effort)

劲头	jìntóu	(名) strength; energy 2 vigour; spirit; drive; zeal
斑纹	bānwén	(名) stripe; streak
激情	jīqíng	(名) strong emotion; enthusiasm

昏迷	hūnmí	(名) stupor; coma:
作风	zuòfēng	(名) style of work; way of life:
科目	kēmù	(名) subject (in a curriculum); course; branch of study
题材	tícái	(名) subject matter; theme:
下属	xiàshǔ	(名) subordinate
补贴	bǔtiē	(名) subsidy; allowance:
实质	shízhì	(名) substance ; essence :
总和	zǒnghé	(名) sum; total; sum total
纪要	jìyào	(名) summary of minutes; summary:
夏令营	xiàlìngyíng	(名) summer camp
神仙	shénxiān	(名) supernatural being; immortal
迷信	míxìn	(名) superstition:
周边	zhōubiān	(名) Surrounding; Neighboring; Periphery
嫌疑	xiányí	(名) suspicion:
武侠	wǔxiá	(名) swordman
符号	fúhào	(名) symbol; mark; sign:
对称	duìchèn	(名) symmetry

症状　　　　　zhèngzhuàng　　　　(名) symptom (any feeling of illness or physical or mental change that is caused by a particular disease)

体系　　　　　tǐxì　　　　(名) system; set-up

策略　　　　　cèlüè　　　　(名) tactics (形) tactful

裁缝　　　　　cáiféng　　　　(名) tailor; dressmaker

指标　　　　　zhǐbiāo　　　　(名) target; quota; norm:

滋味　　　　　zīwèi　　　　(名) taste; flavour

师范　　　　　shīfàn　　　　(名) teacher-training; pedagogical

技能　　　　　jìnéng　　　　(名) technical ability; occupational skills; mastery of a skill or technique:

技巧　　　　　jìqiǎo　　　　(名) technique

性情　　　　　xìngqíng　　　　(名) temperament (the part of your character that affects your moods and the way you behave); temper (mood or emotional state)

温带　　　　　wēndài　　　　(名) Temperate zones

动态　　　　　dòngtài　　　　(名) tendency; trends; developments

帐篷　　　　　zhàngpéng　　　　(名) tent:

领土　　　　　lǐngtǔ　　　　(名) territory; (an area of) land, or sometimes sea, that is considered as belonging to or connected with a particular country or person

考验　　　　　kǎoyàn　　　　(名) test; trial:

上进心	shàngjìn xīn	(名) the desire for progress
端午节	duānwǔ jié	(名) the Dragon Boat Festival (the 5th day of the 5th lunar month)
赤道	chìdào	(名) the equator
正月	zhēngyuè	(名) the first month of the lunar year:
四肢	sìzhī	(名) the four limbs; arms and legs
人间	rénjiān	(名) the human world; man's world; the world:
元宵节	yuánxiāo jié	(名) The Lantern Festival
群众	qúnzhòng	(名) the masses (the ordinary people who form the largest group in a society)
极限	jíxiàn	(名) the maximum; the limit
心灵	xīnlíng	(名) the mind; the soul
须知	xūzhī	(名) the musts:
名副其实	míngfùqíshí	(名) the name matches the reality; be sth. in reality as well as in name; be worthy of the name
北极	běijí	(名) the North Pole; the Arctic Pole
名额	míng'é	(名) the number of people assigned or allowed:
繁体字	fántǐ zì	(名) the original complex form of a simplified Chinese character

| 籍贯 | jíguàn | (名) the place of one's birth or origin |

真相 Zhēnxiàng (名) the real (or true) situation; the real (or actual) facts; the actual state of affairs; truth:

| 夕阳 | xīyáng | (名) the setting sun |

| 国务院 | guówùyuàn | (名) the State Council |

农历 nónglì (名) the traditional Chinese calendar; the lunar calendar

| 翼 | yì | (名) the wing of a bird, aeroplane, etc |

| 主题 | zhǔtí | (名) theme; subject: |

| 学说 | xuéshuō | (名) theory; doctrine |

| 贼 | zéi | (名) thief; burglar |

| 季军 | jìjūn | (名) third place (in a sports contest) |

| 刺 | cì | (名) thorn; splinter (动) prick; stab |

| 思维 | sīwéi | (名) thought; thinking; cognitive; mind |

| 喉咙 | hóulóng | (名) throat |

终年 zhōngnián (名) throughout the year; 2 the age at which one dies

工夫 gōngfū (名) time 2 effort; work; labour 3 workmanship; skill; art

时差	shíchā	(名) time difference; jet lag
梢	shāo	(名) tip; the end of a twig, etc.:
称号	chēnghào	(名) title; designation
标题	biāotí	(名) title; heading; headline; caption:
玩意儿	wányì er	(名) toy; plaything
踪迹	zōngjī	(名) trace; track
田径	tiánjìng	(名) track and field:
商标	shāngbiāo	(名) trade mark.
思绪	sīxù	(名) train of thought; thinking 2 mood
过渡	guòdù	(名) transition
圈套	quāntào	(名) trap
条约	tiáoyuē	(名) treaty; pact
支流	zhīliú	(名) tributary (a river or stream that flows into a larger river or a lake)
把戏	bǎ xì	(名) trick
故障	gùzhàng	(名) trouble; something wrong (with a machine):
后顾之忧	hòugùzhīyōu	(名) troubles back at home; the worries behind
肿瘤	zhǒngliú	(名) tumour:

隧道	suìdào	(名) tunnel; underground passage
动荡	dòngdàng	(名) turbulence; upheaval; unrest
双胞胎	shuāngbāotāi	(名) twins
周折	zhōuzhé	(名) twists and turns; many setbacks; a complicated [troublesome] course of development
台风	táifēng	(名) typhoon
典型	diǎnxíng	(名) typical case of model
轮胎	lúntāi	(名) tyre
制服	zhìfú	(名) uniform
上游	shàngyóu	(名) upper reaches (of a river)
惯例	guànlì	(名) usual practice; convention:
虚荣	xūróng	(名) vainty:
素食主义	sùshí zhǔyì	(名) vegetarianism; doctrine of vegetarian
摊儿	tān er	(名) vendor's stand; booth; stall:
纵横	zònghéng	(名) vertical and horizontal (形) vertically and horizontally; in length and breadth
容器	róngqì	(名) vessel; container
胜负	shèng fù	(名) victory or defeat; success or failure:
见解	jiànjiě	(名) view; opinion; understanding;

生机	shēngjī	(名) vigor (strength, energy, or enthusiasm)
干劲	gànjìng	(名) vigour; drive; enthusiasm (to work)
活力	huólì	(名) vigour；vitality；energy:
别墅	biéshù	(名) villa
乡镇	xiāngzhèn	(名) villages and towns
暴力	bàolì	(名) violence; force; brute force
视力	shìlì	(名) vision; sight
维生素	wéishēngsù	(名) vitamin
词汇	cíhuì	(名) vocabulary
拐杖	guǎizhàng	(名) walking stick; crutches
仓库	cāngkù	(名) warehouse; storehouse:
瀑布	pùbù	(名) waterfall
波浪	bōlàng	(名) wave
出路	chūlù	(名) way out; outlet
途径	tújìng	(名) way; channel:
弱点	ruòdiǎn	(名) weakness; weak point
财富	cáifù	(名) wealth:

分量	fēnliàng	(名) weight; portions; influence; power; weighty

(same as 份量)

福利	fúlì	(名) welfare: well-being:
井	jǐng	(名) well (a deep hole in the ground from which

you can get water, oil, or gas)

码头	mǎtóu	(名) wharf; dock; pier
心得	xīndé	(名) what one has learned from work or study
见闻	jiànwén	(名) what one sees and hears; knowledge; informa

tion :

岳父	yuèfù	(名) wife's father; father-in-law
野心	yěxīn	(名) wild ambition; careerism:
意志	yìzhì	(名) will; will power:
毅力	yìlì	(名) willpower; will; stamina:
风暴	fēngbào	(名) windstorm; storm
眼色	yǎnsè	(名) wink (to close one eye for a short time as a

way of greeting someone or showing friendliness, sexual interest, etc., or of
showing that you are not serious about something you have said)

著作	zhùzuò	(名) works; writings
世界观	shìjièguān	(名) world outlook
顾虑	gùlǜ	(名) worry; misgivings; apprehension:

皱纹　　　　Zhòuwén　　　　(名) wrinkles; lines:

年度　　　　niándù　　　　(名) year （a period of twelve months relating to a particular activity); annual

岁月　　　　suìyuè　　　　(名) years:

亭　　　　tíng　　　　(名)(亭子) pavilion; kiosk:

版本　　　　bǎnběn　　　　(名) edition

2 Verb 动词 dòngcí

HSK 1 Verb 动词 dòngcí (36)

谢谢　　　　xièxiè　　　　(动) thanks; thank you

不客气　　　　bù kèqì

2 (in reply to one's thanks) you're welcome; don't mention it; not at all

再见　　　　zàijiàn　　　　(套) goodbye; see you again

请　　　　qǐng　　　2[9] (敬) please:

对不起　　duìbùqǐ　　1 (套) I' m sorry; excuse me; pardon me; I beg your

pardon

没关系　　méiguānxì　　it doesn't matter; it's nothing; that's all right; never mind

是　　　　shì　　　　1 (动) [used as the verb to be when the predicative is a

noun] :

有　　　　yǒu　　　　1 (动) have; possess

---

[9] The number 2 here indicates the second meaning. One Chines Character may have many meanings. A phrase can related to many meanings. This is the hard part of Chinese language. So, pay attention to the Shape of Chinese Characters, at least you can read out or know the meaning, will help you a lot in your Chinese learning journey. i.e 请　qǐng　　1 (动) treat

请客　qǐngkè play the host; stand treat

请　　qǐng　　2 (敬) please:

请坐　qǐng zuò　　　(动) Please sit; Please take a seat

请　　qǐng　　hire

聘请　pìnqǐng　　　(动) invite; hire

请　　Qǐng　　3.(招待; 款待) entertain

我们请朋友吃午饭。　　　wǒmen qǐng péngyǒu chī wǔfàn.　　　we entertained friends to lunch.

请　　Qǐng　　4.[敬] (用于希望对方做某事) please

请安静。　qǐng ānjìng.　　be quiet, please.

看	kàn	1 (动) see; look at ; watch:
听	tīng	1 (动) listen; hear:
说话	shuōhuà	1 (动) speak; talk; say:
读	dú	1 (动) read; read aloud :
写	xiě	(动) write
看见	kànjiàn	(动) catch sight of; see
叫	jiào	4 name; call:
来	Lái	1 (动) come; arrive:
回	huí	1 (动) return; go back:
去	qù	1 (动) go; leave
吃	chī	(动) 1 eat; take:
喝	hē	(动) 1 drink:
睡觉	shuìjiào	(动) sleep:
打电话	dǎ diànhuà	make a phone call.

做	zuò	(动) 1 do:
买	mǎi	(动) buy; purchase:
开	kāi	1 (动) open:
坐	zuò	1 (动) sit:
住	zhù	1(动) live; reside; stay
学习	xuéxí	(动) study; learn
工作	gōngzuò	1 (名) work; job:
下雨	xià yǔ	raining
爱	ài	1 love:
喜欢	xǐhuān	1 (动) like; love; be fond of
想	xiǎng	1 (动) think:
认识	rènshí	1 (动) know; recognize:
会	Huì	3 can; be able to:
能	néng	1 (动) can; be able to:

卖	mài	1 (动) sell:
问	wèn	1 (动) ask; inquire:
走	zǒu	1 (动) walk:
进	jìn	(动) 2 enter; come or go into:
出	chū	1 (动) 1 go or come out:
跑步	pǎobù	(动) run
到	dào	(动) 1 arrive; reach
穿	chuān	(动) 1 wear; put on:
洗	xǐ	1 (动) , wash:
给	gěi	1 (动) give:
找	zhǎo	1 (动) look for; try to find; seek:

懂	dǒng	(动) understand; know:
笑	xiào	1 (动) smile; laugh:
回答	huídá	(动) answer; reply
告诉	gàosù	(动) tell; let know:
准备	zhǔnbèi	1 (动) prepare:
开始	kāishǐ	1 (动) begin; start:
介绍	jièshào	1 (动) introduce; present:
帮助	bāngzhù	help; assist:
玩	wán	1 (动) play; have fun:
送	sòng	1 (动) delivery; carry

等	děng	3 (动) wait; await:
让	ràng	4 let; allow:

起床	qǐchuáng	(动) get up (from bed)
唱歌	chànggē	sing a song
跳舞	tiàowǔ	(动) dance
旅游	lǚyóu	(动) tour:
上班	shàngbān	(动) go to work; start work; be on duty:
生病	shēngbìng	(动) fall ill
休息	xiūxí	(动) rest:
运动	yùndòng	(动) 3 do sports; do exercise:

游泳	yóuyǒng	(动) swim:
踢足球	tī zúqiú	(动) play football
打篮球	dǎ lánqiú	(动) play basketball.
完	wán	2 (动) run out; use up:
觉得	juédé	1 (动) feel:
知道	zhīdào	(动) know; be aware of; realize:
希望	xīwàng	1 (动) hope; wish; expect:
可以	kěyǐ	1 (动) can; may:
要	yào	(动) 5 want; desire:
可能	kěnéng	1 (形) possible; probable:

HSK 3 Verb 动词 dòngcí (78)

锻炼   duànliàn   (动) 1 take physical exercise

发现   fāxiàn   (动) find; discover

发烧   fāshāo   (动) run a fever; have a temperature

放   fàng   (动) 1 put; place:

放心   fàngxīn   动) feel relieved; set one's mind at rest; be at ease:

复习   fùxí   (动 review; revise:

敢   gǎn   1 (动) dare:

关   guān   1 (动) shut; close:

关心   guānxīn   (动) be concerned about; concern oneself with; pay great attention to:

害怕   hàipà   (动) fear; be afraid; be scared:

还   huán   2 (动) give back; return; repay:

换   huàn   2 (动) change:

记得   jì dé   (动) remember:

检查	jiǎnchá	1 (动) check; inspect; examine:
见面	jiànmiàn	(动) meet; see;
讲	jiǎng	1 (动) speak; say; tell:
教	jiāo	(动) teach; instruct
接	jiē	(动) 3 catch; take hold of:
结束	jiéshù	(动) end; finish ; conclude; wind up; close:
搬	bān	1 (动) take away; move; remove:
解决	jiějué	1 (动) solve; resolve; settle:
借	jiè	1 (动) borrow:

经过	jīngguò	1 (动) , pass; go through; undergo:
举行	jǔxíng	(动 hold (a meeting, ceremony, etc.):
哭	kū	(动) cry; weep; sob:
帮忙	bāngmáng	(动) help; give (or lend) a hand; do a favour
离开	líkāi	(动) leave; depart; go away
了解	liǎojiě	1 (动) know; understand:
饱	bǎo	1 (动) have eaten one's fill; be full:

满意　　　　mǎnyì　　　　(动) be satisfied (形) satisfied; pleased:

对...满意　　duì... Mǎnyì　　　Be satisfied with…

明白　　　　míngbái　　　1 (形) clear; obvious; plain:

问题讲得很明白　　wèntí jiǎng dé hěn míngbái

The problem is clearly expounded.

明白　　　　míngbái　　　4 (动) understand; realize; know:

你明白我的意思吗？　nǐ míngbái wǒ de yìsi ma?　　Do you see what I mean?

比较　　　　bǐjiào　　　　(动) 1 compare; contrast:

比较　　　　bǐjiào　　　　3 (副) fairly; comparatively; relatively; quite; rather:

我比较喜欢看电影　　wǒ bǐjiào xǐhuān kàn diànyǐng　Relatively speaking, I like films.

难过　　　　nánguò　　　2 (动) feel sad; be grieved:

没关系，别难过，高兴点儿。

Méiguānxì, bié nánguò, gāoxìng diǎn er.

No problem, do not be sad, be happy little bit.

努力　　　　　nǔlì　　　　　（动）try hard; make great efforts; exert oneself:

爬山　　　　　páshān　　　　（动）climb a mountain

必须　　　　　bìxū　　　　　（动）must; have to:

变化　　　　　biànhuà　　　　（动）change; vary:

骑　　　　　　qí　　　　　　（动）ride (esp. on animal or bicycle):

清楚　　　　　qīngchǔ　　　1（形）clear; distinct:

他说话不清楚　　tā shuōhuà bù qīngchǔ　　He doesn't speak distinctly.

清楚 qīngchǔ　　　　　2（动）be clear about; understand:

这件事我不太清楚　　zhè jiàn shì wǒ bù tài qīngchǔ　　I don't know much about the matter.

表示　　　　　biǎoshì　　　　（动）show; express; indicate:

认为　　　　　Rènwéi　　　　（动）think; consider; hold; deem; take for; regard as; look upon as; take sb. [sth.] as; be known as; set down as

表演　　　　　biǎoyǎn　　　　（动）1 perform act; play:

上网	shàng wǎng	(动) be on line; use the internet; have access to the internet
生气	shēngqì	1 (动) take offence; get angry; Pissed off
刷牙	shuāyá	(动) brush one's teeth.
提高	tígāo	(动) raise; heighten; enhance; increase; improve:
同意	tóngyì	(动) agree; consent; approve
完成	wánchéng	(动) accomplish; complete; fulfil; bring to success (or fruition):
忘记	wàngjì	1 (动) forget
洗澡	xǐzǎo	(动) take a bath; swim
相信	xiāngxìn	(动) believe; have faith in
像	xiàng	2 (动) be like; resemble:
爱好	àihào	1 (动) love; like; be keen on: 2 (名) interest; hobby:
需要	xūyào	1 (动) need; require:
选择	xuǎnzé	(动) select; make a choice:
以为	yǐwéi	(动) think; consider; believe; thought so;

应该　　　　yīnggāi　　　(动) Should; Ought to

影响　　　　yǐngxiǎng　　　1 (名) influence; effect:

产生巨大影响　　chǎnshēng jùdà yǐngxiǎng　　　exercise a great influence

影响　　　　yǐngxiǎng　　　2 (动) affect; influence:

影响健康　　yǐngxiǎng jiànkāng　　affect one's health.

用　　　　　yòng　　　1 (动) use; employ; apply

遇到　　　　yù dào　　　(动) meet; run into; encounter; come across:

拿　　　　　ná　　　(动) 2 take; bring:

愿意　　　　Yuànyì　　　1 (动) be willing; be ready; 2 wish; like ; want:

参加　　　　cānjiā　　　(动) join; attend; take part in:

长　　　　　zhǎng　　　3 (动) grow; develop:

着急　　　　zhāojí　　　(动) feel worried:

照顾　　　　zhàogù　　　(动) 2 look after; care for; attend to:

祝　　　　　zhù　　　(动) offer good wishes; wish:

注意	zhùyì	(动) pay attention to; take notice of:
迟到	chídào	(动) be late:

出现	chūxiàn	(动) appear; emerge :
打扫	dǎsǎo	(动) clean; sweep:
打算	dǎsuàn	(动) 1 plan; intend

带	dài	4 (动) take; bring; carry:
带上雨衣	dài shàng yǔyī	Take your raincoat along.

担心	dānxīn	(动) worry; feel anxious:
决定	juédìng	1 (动) decide; resolve; make up one's mind
信	xìn	4 (动) believe; trust:
要求	yāoqiú	(动) ask for; demand ; request:
站	zhàn	1 (动) stand; be on one's feet:

HSK 4 Verb 动词 dòngcí (188)

失望	shīwàng	(动)[10] be disappointed
安排	ānpái	(动) arrange; plan; fix up:
按照	ànzhào	(动) according to; in accordance with; in the light of; on the basis of:
抱	bào	(动) hold or carry in one's arms; embrace; hug
报道	bàodào	(动) report (news); cover:
保护	bǎohù	(动) protect ; safeguard :
包括	bāokuò	(动) include; consist of; comprise; incorporate :
报名	bàomíng	(动) enter one's name; sign up
抱歉	bàoqiàn	(动) be sorry; regret:
保证	bǎozhèng	(动) pledge; guarantee; assure; ensure
表达	biǎodá	(动) express (thoughts and feelings)
表扬	biǎoyáng	(动) praise; commend
毕业	bìyè	(动) graduate; finish school:
不管	bùguǎn	(动) no matter (what, how, etc.) ; regardless of:
擦	cā	(动) clean; wipe

[10] (动) indicates 动词 dòngcí   Verb

猜	cāi	(动) guess; speculate
参观	cānguān	(动) visit (place, exhibition, etc.)
尝	cháng	(动) taste; experience:
吵	chǎo	(动) make a noise
超过	chāoguò	(动) outstrip; surpass; exceed
成功	chénggōng	(动) succeed
成为	chéngwéi	(动) become; turn into:
乘坐	chéngzuò	(动) travel by
吃惊	chījīng	(动) be startled; be shocked; be amazed; be taken aback:
抽烟	chōuyān	(动) smoke (a cigarette or a pipe)
出差	chūchāi	(动) be on a business trip
出发	chūfā	(动) set out; start off:
出生	chūshēng	(动) be born:
打扮	dǎbàn	(动) dress up; make up; deck out
戴	dài	(动) wear （accessories, such as hat, watches, rings, necklace etc.)
代替	dàitì	(动) replace; substitute (for); take the place of
弹钢琴	tán gāngqín	(动) play the piano

道歉	dàoqiàn	(动) apologize
打扰	dǎrǎo	(动) disturb
打印	dǎyìn	(动) to print (using printer)
打折	dǎzhé	(动) sell at a discount; give a discount
打针	dǎzhēn	(动) give or receive an injection
得	dé	(动) get; gain; obtain:
掉	diào	(动) fall; drop;
调查	diàochá	(动) investigate; survey:
丢	diū	(动) lose; be missed
断	duàn	(动) break; snap; cut:
发	fā	(动) send out; issue; dispatch; distribute:
反对	fǎnduì	(动) be against
放暑假	fàng shǔjià	(动) have summer vacation (or holidays)
放弃	fàngqì	(动) abandon; give up; renounce:
访问	fǎngwèn	(动) visit; call on
翻译	fānyì	(动) translate; interpret:
反映	fǎnyìng	(动) reflect; mirror; portray; depict :
发生	fāshēng	(动) happen; occur; take place

发展	fāzhǎn	(动) 1 develop; expand; grow:
丰富	fēngfù	(动) enrich
符合	fúhé	(动) accord with: conform to; be in line with:
复印	fùyìn	(动) photocopy; duplicate; xerox
负责	fùzé	(动) be responsible for; be in charge of:
改变	gǎibiàn	(动) change; alter; transform:
干	gàn	(动) do; work:
干杯	gānbēi	(动) drink a toast; cheers
感动	gǎndòng	(动) move; touch:
感谢	gǎnxiè	(动) thank; be grateful:
购物	gòuwù	(动) go shopping; purchase:
挂	guà	(动) hang; put up; suspend:
逛	guàng	(动) stroll; roam:
估计	gūjì	(动) estimate ; appraise; reckon:
鼓励	gǔlì	(动) encourage; urge
过	guò	(动) pass; cross:
鼓掌	gǔzhǎng	(动) clap one's hands; applaud:
好像	hǎoxiàng	(动) seem; be like:

后悔	hòuhuǐ	(动) regret; repent:
花	huā	(动) spend (time, money); expend
怀疑	huáiyí	(动) suspect; be suspicious of (名) doubt; suspect
获得	huòdé	(动) gain; obtain; acquire; win; achieve:
寄	jì	(动) send; post; mail:
加班	jiābān	(动) work overtime; work an extra shift:
坚持	jiānchí	(动) persist ln; persevere in; uphold; insist on; stick to; adhere to:
减肥	jiǎnféi	(动) reduce weight; slim:
降低	jiàngdī	(动) reduce; cut down; drop; lower:
减少	jiǎnshǎo	(动) reduce; decrease; lessen; cut down:
交	jiāo	(动) associate with:
解释	jiěshì	(动) explain; expound; interpret :
接受	jiēshòu	(动) accept:
节约	jiéyuē	(动) practise economy; economize; save:
集合	jíhé	(动) gather; assemble; muster; call together:
积累	jīlěi	(动) accumulate; (名) accumulation
进行	jìnxíng	(动) be on the march; march; advance:

禁止	jìnzhǐ	(动) prohibit; ban; forbid:
继续	jìxù	(动) continue; go on:
举办	jǔbàn	(动) conduct; hold; run:
拒绝	jùjué	(动) refuse:
开玩笑	kāiwánxiào	(动) crack a joke; joke; make fun of; play a joke (or prank) on; make jests
考虑	kǎolǜ	(动) think over; consider:
肯定	kěndìng	(动) affirm; confirm; approve; regard as positive:
咳嗽	késòu	(动) cough
扩大	kuòdà	(动) enlarge; expand; extend:
拉	lā	(动) pull; draw; tug; drag
来不及	láibují	(动) there's not enough time (to do sth.); it's too late (to do sth.):
来得及	láidéjí	(动) there's s till time; be able to do sth. in time; be able to make it:
浪费	làngfèi	(动) waste; squander:
联系	liánxì	(动) contact; get in touch with; link:
聊天儿	liáotiān er	(动) (口)[11] chat

---

[11] (口)   indicates Oral or Spoken

理发	lǐfǎ	(动) have a haircu; (名) haircut
理解	lǐjiě	(动) understand; comprehend:
例如	lìrú	(动) for instance; for example (e. g.); such as
留	liú	(动) remain ; stay:
流泪	liúlèi	(动) shed tears
留学	liúxué	(动) study abroad:
弄	nòng	(动) do; make; handle; manage; get:
排列	páiliè	(动) put in order; rank:
判断	pànduàn	(动) judge; decide; determine:
陪	péi	(动) accompany; keep sb. company:
骗	piàn	(动) deceive; fool; hoodwink:
批评	pīpíng	(动) criticize
破	pò	(动) break; split; cleave; cut (形) broken; damaged ; torn; worn-out:
敲	qiāo	(动) knock; beat; strike:
起飞	qǐfēi	(动) (of aircraft) take off:
起来	qǐlái	(动) get up; rise; arouse:
请假	qǐngjià	(动) ask for leave.

请客	qǐngkè	(动) stand treat; entertain guests; give a dinner party; play the host
取	qǔ	(动) take; get; fetch:
区别	qūbié	(动) distinguish:
缺少	quēshǎo	(动) lack; be short of:
扔	rēng	(动) throw; toss; cast:
散步	sànbù	(动) take a walk
商量	shāngliáng	(动) consult; discuss; talk over:
剩	shèng	(动) be left (over); remain:
试	shì	(动) try; test:
适应	shìyìng	(动) suit ; adapt ; fit :
使用	shǐyòng	(动) make use of; use; employ; apply:
收	shōu	(动) recieve; accept:
受不了	shòu bù liǎo	(动) cannot stand it
受到	shòudào	(动) receive; accept:
收拾	shōushí	(动) tidy up.
输	shū	(动) lose; be beaten; be defeated:
说明	shuōmíng	(动) explain; illustrate:

熟悉	shúxī	(动)(书) be familiar with; be good at
死	sǐ	(动) die
算	suàn	(动) calculate
抬	tái	(动) (of two or more people) carry:
谈	tán	(动) talk，chat; discuss:
躺	tǎng	(动) lie; recline:
讨厌	tǎoyàn	(动) dislike; loathe; hate; be disgusted with
填空	tiánkòng	(动) Fill in the blank
提供	tígōng	(动) provide; supply; furnish; offer:
停止	Tíngzhǐ	(动) stop; cease; halt; suspend; call off:
提前	tíqián	(动) do sth. in advance or ahead of time:
提醒	tíxǐng	(动) remind; warn; call attention to:
通过	tōngguò	(动) pass through; pass:
同情	tóngqíng	(动) sympathize with; show sympathy for:
推	tuī	(动) push; shove:
推迟	tuīchí	(动) put off; postpone; defer:
脱	tuō	(动) (of hair, skin) peel off;
握手	wòshǒu	(动) shake hands

无	wú	(动) not have; there is not; without:
误会	wùhuì	(动) misunderstand; mistake; misconstrue:
羡慕	xiànmù	(动) admire; envy
限制	xiànzhì	(动) restrict; limit; confine:
行	xíng	(动) walk; travel 2 prevail: 3 do; carry out:
醒	xǐng	(动) wake up
信任	xìnrèn	(动) trust; have confidence in
修	xiū	(动) repair:
吸引	xīyǐn	(动) attract; draw; fascinate:
演出	yǎnchū	(动) perform; show; put on a show:
养成	yǎng chéng	(动) form; acquire; cultivate:
邀请	yāoqǐng	(动) invite (usu. for certain specific purposes)
赢	yíng	(动) win; beat:
引起	yǐnqǐ	(动) give rise to; lead to; cause; arouse:
原谅	yuánliàng	(动) excuse; forgive; pardon
允许	yǔnxǔ	(动) permit; allow
预习	yùxí	(动) study in advance; pre study

增加	zēngjiā	(动) increase; raise; add:
增长	zēngzhǎng	(动) increase; rise; grow:
招聘	zhāopìn	(动) advertise for (workers, teachers, etc.)
整理	zhěnglǐ	(动) put in order; straighten out; arrange; sort out:
证明	zhèngmíng	(动) prove; testify; bear out
指	zhǐ	(动) point to; point at
支持	zhīchí	(动) support; back; espouse:
值得	zhídé	(动) be of value:
制造	zhìzào	(动) make; manufacture:
重视	zhòngshì	(动) attach importance to; pay attention to:
赚	zhuàn	(动) make a profit; gain:
撞	zhuàng	(动) hit；strike；bump；shove；run in
祝贺	Zhùhè	(动) congratulate :
总结	zǒngjié	(动) sum up; summarize:
租	zū	(动) rent: hire: lease: let:
组成	zǔchéng	(动) make up; compose; consist of:
尊重	zūnzhòng	(动) treat with respect; value:
做生意	zuò shēngyì	(动) do business

阅读	yuèdú	(动) read:

HSK 5 Verb 动词 dòngcí (455)

分布	fēnbù	(动) distribute; spread; scatter:
晒	shài	(动) (of the sun) shine upon 2 dry in the sun; bask
针对	zhēnduì	(动) be directed against; be aimed at:
等于	děngyú	(动) be equal to; be equivalent to:
咬	yǎo	(动) bite; snap at:
摸	mō	(动) feel; stroke; touch
成立	chénglì	(动) set up; found; establish:
传播	chuánbò	(动) spread；disseminate; propagate
蹲	dūn	(动) squat
念	niàn	(动) think of; miss:
劳驾	láojià	(动) (套) [polite form used when one requests people to make way. etc.] excuse me; may I trouble you:

采访	cǎifǎng	(动) (of a reporter) gather material; cover:
占线	zhànxiàn	(动) (of a telephone line) in use:
嫁	jià	(动) (of a woman) marry (out)
去世	qùshì	(动) (of grown-up people) die; pass away
涨	zhǎng	(动) (of water level, prices, etc.) rise; go up
出口	chūkǒu	(动) (名) export (名) exit
微笑	wéixiào	(动) (名) smile
答应	dāyìng	(动) 1 answer; reply; respond 2 promise; agree
称	chēng	(动) 1 call; address 2 weigh; scale (名) name
背	bèi	(动) 1 carry on one's back 2 bear; shoulder
提	tí	(动) 1 carry; 2 mention; refer to; bring up
指挥	zhǐhuī	(动) 1 command; direct; conduct 2 (名) commander; director; conductor
收获	shōuhuò	(动) 1 gather (or bring) in the crops; harvest 2 (名) results; gains
除	chú	(动) 1 get rid of; do away with; remove
从事	cóngshì	(动) 1 go in for; be engaged in:
装	zhuāng	(动) 1 install; fit 2 fill; load 3 pretend; feign (名) clothing; outfit

漏	lòu	(动) 1 leak 2 divulge; leak
移动	yídòng	(动) 1 move; remove; shift: 2 change; alter:
欠	qiàn	(动) 1 owe 2 short of; lacking
滚	gǔn	(动) 1 roll 2 Get away 3 boil
扶	fú	(动) 1 support with the hand:
翻	fān	(动) 1 turn (over, up, upside down, etc.) 2 translate:
劳动	láodòng	(动) 1 work; labour: 2 do physical labour; do manual labour
吸收	xīshōu	(动) absorb; assimilate; imbibe
应聘	yìngpìn	(动) accept an offer of employment:
达到	dádào	(动) achieve; attain; reach:
调整	tiáozhěng	(动) adjust; regulate; revise:
佩服	pèifú	(动) admire:
承认	chéngrèn	(动) admit; acknowledge; recognize:
采取	cǎiqǔ	(动) adopt; take:

进步	jìnbù	(动) advance; progress; improve:
劝	quàn	(动) advise; urge:
提倡	tíchàng	(动) advocate; encourage:
分配	fēnpèi	(动) allocate ; assign; distribute:
分析	fēnxī	(动) analyze:
钓	diào	(动) angle; fish with hook and bait
应用	yìngyòng	(动) apply; use:
评价	píngjià	(动) appraise; evaluate:
赞成	zànchéng	(动) approve of; assent; agree with; give one's blessing to:
批准	pīzhǔn	(动) approve; endorse; sanction:
热爱	rè'ài	(动) ardent love
辩论	biànlùn	(动) argue; debate:
争论	zhēnglùn	(动) argue; dispute
启发	qǐfā	(动) arouse; inspire; enlighten:
到达	dàodá	(动) arrive; get to; reach
打听	dǎtīng	(动) ask about; inquire about:

请求	qǐngqiú	(动) ask; request:
承担	chéngdān	(动) assume; undertake:
出席	chūxí	(动) attend; be present (at a meeting, banquet, etc.)
避免	bìmiǎn	(动) avoid; refrain from; avert:
拦	lán	(动) bar; block; hold back:
接近	jiējìn	(动) be close to; near; approach
自信	zìxìn	(动) be confident :
自觉	zìjué	(动) be conscious of
面临	miànlín	(动) be faced with; be confronted with; be up against:
空闲	kòngxián	(动) be free:
体贴	tǐtiē	(动) be full of thought for:
善于	shànyú	(动) be good at; be adept in:
主持	zhǔchí	(动) be in charge of
受伤	shòushāng	(动) be injured; be wounded; sustain an injury
相关	xiāngguān	(动) be interrelated:
舍不得	shěbudé	(动) be not willing to give away; grudge:
讲究	jiǎngjiù	(动) be particular about; pay attention to; stress; strive for:
上当	shàngdàng	(动) be taken in

疼爱	téng'ài	(动) be very fond of; love very dearly
承受	chéngshòu	(动) bear; sustain; withstand; endure:
属于	shǔyú	(动) belong to; be part of:
弯	wān	(动) bend; flex:
挡	dǎng	(动) block; keep
吹	chuī	(动) blow; exhale:
煮	zhǔ	(动) boil; cook
碎	suì	(动) break to pieces; smash (形) broken
哈	hā	(动) breathe out (with the mouth open)
呼吸	Hūxī	(动) breathe; respire :
建设	jiànshè	(动) build; construct (名) 2 construction
建筑	jiànzhú	(动) build; construct; erect:
燃烧	ránshāo	(动) burn
称呼	chēnghu	(动) call; address:
取消	qǔxiāo	(动) cancel; abolish:
执行	zhíxíng	(动) carry out; execute ; implement:
着凉	zháoliáng	(动) catch cold
庆祝	qìngzhù	(动) celebrate :

挑战	tiǎozhàn	(动) challenge:
怀念	huáiniàn	(动) cherish the memory of:
爱护	àihù	(动) cherish; treasure; protect:
教训	jiàoxùn	(动) chide; teach sb. a lesson; give sb. a dressing down; lecture sb. (for wrongdoing, etc.) 2 (名) lesson; moral
拍	pāi	(动) clap; pat; beat:
关闭	guānbì	(动) close; shut
辅导	fǔdǎo	(动) coach; give tutorials to:
结合	jiéhé	(动) combine; unite; integrate; link:
来自	láizì	(动) come from
开放	kāifàng	(动) come into bloom:
接触	jiēchù	(动) come mto contact with; get in touch with
安慰	ānwèi	(动) comfort; console
纪念	jìniàn	(动) commemorate; mark (名) souvenir; keepsake; memento
议论	yìlùn	(动) comment; talk; discuss:
赔偿	péicháng	(动) compensate; pay for:
集中	jízhōng	(动) concentrate; centralize; focus; amass; put together:

操心	cāoxīn	(动) concern; worry about; take pains:
确认	quèrèn	(动) Confirm; afirm; verify
参考	cānkǎo	(动) consult; refer to:
消费	xiāofèi	(动) consume (名) consumption
持续	chíxù	(动) continue; sustain:
对比	duìbǐ	(动) contrast; compare:
贡献	gòngxiàn	(动) contribute; dedicate; devote (名) contribution
捐	juān	(动) contribute; donate; subscribe:
控制	kòngzhì	(动) control; dominate; command:
召开	zhàokāi	(动) convene; convoke:
合作	hézuò	(动) cooperate; collaborate; work together:
配合	pèihé	(动) coordinate; cooperate:
抄	chāo	(动) copy; transcribe:
改正	gǎizhèng	(动) correct; amend; put right:
相当	xiāngdāng	(动) correspond to; be equal to (副) quite; considerably:
计算	jìsuàn	(动) count; compute; calculate: (名) consideration; planning:
创造	chuàngzào	(动) create; produce:

拥挤	yǒngjǐ	(动) crowd; push and squeeze
砍	kǎn	(动) cut; chop; hack:
切	qiē	(动) cut; slice:
宣布	xuānbù	(动) declare; proclaim; announce:
推辞	tuīcí	(动) decline (an appointment , invitation, etc.)
装饰	zhuāngshì	(动) decorate ; adorn:
油炸	yóu zhá	(动) deep-fry
删除	shānchú	(动) delete; strike (or cut, cross) out
否认	fǒurèn	(动) deny
降落	jiàngluò	(动) descend; land:
形容	xíngróng	(动) describe:
描写	miáoxiě	(动) describe; depict; portray
破坏	pòhuài	(动) destroy; wreck; undermine; sabotage:
开发	kāifā	(动) develop; open up; exploit:
诊断	zhěnduàn	(动) diagnose:
消化	xiāohuà	(动) digest (名) digestion
导演	dǎoyǎn	(动) direct (a film, play, etc.) (名) director
消失	xiāoshī	(动) disappear

宣传	xuānchuán	(动) disseminate; publicize; propagate:
分别	fēnbié	(动) distinguish; differentiate 3 (副) differently:
离婚	líhūn	(动) divorce
尽力	jìnlì	(动) do all one can; try one's best:
营业	yíngyè	(动) do business:
搞	gǎo	(动) do; make:
下载	xiàzài	(动) download
披	pī	(动) drape over one's shoulders:
驾驶	jiàshǐ	(动) drive (a vehicle); pilot (a ship or plane):
复制	fùzhì	(动) duplicate; reproduce; copy:
挣钱	zhèng qián	(动) earn money; earn a living; make money
节省	jiéshěng	(动) economize; save; use sparingly; cut down on:
编辑	biānjí	(动) edit; compile (名) 2 editor; compiler
选举	xuǎnjǔ	(动) elect; vote
消灭	xiāomiè	(动) eliminate; wipe out:
体现	tǐxiàn	(动) embody; incarnate; reflect; give expression to:
拥抱	yǒngbào	(动) embrace; hug
雇佣	gùyōng	(动) employ; hire:

嘱咐	zhǔfù	(动) enjoin; exhort:
享受	xiǎngshòu	(动) enjoy:
欣赏	xīnshǎng	(动) enjoy; appreciate; admire
录取	lùqǔ	(动) enrol; recruit; admit:
招待	zhāodài	(动) entertain; serve (customers) :
委托	wěituō	(动) entrust; trust:
逃避	táobì	(动) escape; evade; shirk:
建交	jiànjiāo	(动) establish diplomatic relations
赞美	zànměi	(动) eulogize; praise
夸	kuā	(动) exaggerate; overstate; boast:
交换	jiāohuàn	(动) exchange; swop:
使劲儿	shǐjìn er	(动) exert all one's strength:
存在	cúnzài	(动) exist:
过期	guòqí	(动) expire; be overdue:
相对	xiāngduì	(动) face each other (副) relatively; comparatively:
面对	miàn duì	(动) facing to
落后	luòhòu	(动) fall behind; lag behind:
倒	dào	(动) fall; topple:

摔	shuāi	(动) fall; tumble; lose one's balance
		2 cast ; throw; fling
满足	mǎnzú	(动) feel content; feel satisfied:
晕	yūn	(动) feel dizzy; feel giddy
感激	gǎnjī	(动) feel grateful; be thankful; feel indebted:
开心	kāixīn	(动) feel happy; rejoice
委屈	wěiqu	(动) feel wronged; nurse a grievance:
奋斗	fèndòu	(动) fight to achieve a goal; struggle; strive:
充满	chōngmǎn	(动) fill; be filled with
不好意思	bù hǎoyìsi	(动) find it embarrassing (to do sth.):
罚款	fákuǎn	(动) fine (to charge someone an amount of money

as a punishment for not obeying a rule or law) (名) penalty, fine

确定	quèdìng	(动) fix; determine; decide on
固定	gùdìng	(动) fix; regularize:
飘	piāo	(动) float (in the air); flutter :
接着	Jiēzhe	(动) follow; carry on (副) then, following on
比如	bǐrú	(动) for example; for instance; such as

预报	yùbào	(动) forecast:
构成	gòuchéng	(动) form; constitute; make up:
冻	dòng	(动) freeze
煎	jiān	(动) fry in shallow oil:
相处	xiāngchǔ	(动) get along (with one another) :
迷路	mílù	(动) get lost (the way)
聚会	jùhuì	(动) get together; meet:
治疗	zhìliáo	(动) give medical treatment to a patient
发挥	fāhuī	(动) give play to; bring into play:
戒烟	jièyān	(动) give up smoking .
浏览	liúlǎn	(动) glance over; skim through (or over); browse through
破产	pòchǎn	(动) go bankrupt (名) bankruptcy
游览	yóulǎn	(动) go sightseeing; tour
掌握	zhǎngwò	(动) grasp; master; know well:
打招呼	dǎzhāohū	(动) greet sb. (by word or gesture)
成长	chéngzhǎng	(动) grow up
指导	zhǐdǎo	(动) guide; direct:

递	dì	(动) hand over; pass; give:
处理	chǔlǐ	(动) handle; attend to; dispose of:
办理	bànlǐ	(动) handle; conduct; transact:
危害	wéihài	(动) harm; endanger; jeopardize:
协调	xiétiáo	(动) harmonize; coordinate:
恨	hèn	(动) hate:
一路平安!	yīlù píng'ān!	(动) Have a good trip! or Bon voyage!
歇	xiē	(动) have a rest:
倒霉	dǎoméi	(动) have bad luck; get into trouble
打交道	dǎjiāodào	(动) have dealings with; come into contact with:
闻	wén	(动) hear:
犹豫	yóuyù	(动) hesitate; waver:
躲藏	duǒcáng	(动) hide (or conceal) oneself; go into hiding
妨碍	fáng'ài	(动) hinder; hamper; impede; obstruct
耽误	dānwù	(动) hinder; hold up; spoil sth. because of delay:
担任	dānrèn	(动) hold the post of; take charge of:
把握	bǎwò	(动) hold; grasp (名) assurance; certainty
主张	zhǔzhāng	(动) hold; maintain; advocate:

盼望	pànwàng	(动) hope for; long for; look forward to:
期待	qídài	(动) hope; expect; look forward to:
催	cuī	(动) hurry; urge; press; speed up:
忽视	hūshì	(动) ignore; overlook; neglect
模仿	mófǎng	(动) imitate; copy; mimic
促使	cùshǐ	(动) impel; spur; encourage:
输入	shūrù	(动) import
进口	jìnkǒu	(动) import (名) entrance
改善	gǎishàn	(动) improve; better:
改进	gǎijìn	(动) improve; make better:
传染	chuánrǎn	(动) infect; be contagious:
询问	xúnwèn	(动) inquire; ask:
鼓舞	gǔwǔ	(动) inspire; hearten:
安装	ānzhuāng	(动) install
侵略	qīnlüè	(动) invade; (名) aggression
发明	fāmíng	(动) invent
投资	tóuzī	(动) invest

烫	tàng	(动) 1 iron; press
		2 (形) very hot; scalding; boiling hot
据说	jùshuō	(动) it is said; they say:
看来	kàn lái	(动) it seems (or appears) ; it looks as if:
痒	yǎng	(动) itch
抓紧	zhuājǐn	(动) keep a firm grasp on:
保持	bǎochí	(动) keep; maintain:
杀	shā	(动) kill; slaughter:
吻	wěn	(动) kiss
体会	tǐhuì	(动) know (or learn) from experience; understand
缺乏	quēfá	(动) lack; be short of:
退步	tuìbù	(动) lag (or fall) behind; retrogress
展开	zhǎnkāi	(动) launch; unfold; develop; carry out:
制定	zhìdìng	(动) lay down; formulate:
牵	qiān	(动) lead along; pull; drag:
导致	dǎozhì	(动) lead to; result in; bring about; cause:
领导	lǐngdǎo	(动) lead; exercise leadership

体验	tǐyàn	(动) learn through practice; learn through one's personal experience :
省略	shěnglüè	(动) leave out; omit:
延长	yáncháng	(动) lengthen; prolong; extend:
解放	jiěfàng	(动) liberate; emancipate:
举	jǔ	(动) lift; raise; hold up:
沟通	gōutōng	(动) link up; connect
度过	dùguò	(动) live through,spend,pass away
轻视	qīngshì	(动) look down on; despise; underestimate
看不起	kànbùqǐ	(动) look down upon; scorn; despise
瞧	qiáo	(动) look; see:
显得	xiǎndé	(动) look; seem; appear:
灰心	huīxīn	(动) lose heart; be discouraged; be disappointed
失业	shīyè	(动) lose one's job; be out of work; be unemployed
失去	shīqù	(动) lose:
损失	sǔnshī	(动) lose:
恋爱	liàn'ài	(动) love; be in love
造成	zàochéng	(动) made, caused;

建议	jiànyì	(动) 1 make a suggestion
		(名) 2 proposal; suggestion; recommendation
应付	yìngfù	(动) make do with sth.
表明 indicate:	biǎomíng	(动) make known; make clear; state clearly;
公布	gōngbù	(动) make public; announce:
组合	zǔhé	(动) make up; compose ; combine
制作	zhìzuò	(动) make; manufacture:
经营	jīngyíng	(动) manage; run; engage in:
生产	shēngchǎn	(动) manufacture:
娶	qǔ	(动) marry (a woman); take to wife:
碰见	pèngjiàn	(动) meet unexpectedly; run into
迎接	yíngjiē	(动) meet; greet:
融化	rónghuà	(动) melt; thaw:
移民	yímín	(动) migrate; emigrate; immigrate
想念	xiǎngniàn	(动) miss sb.
甩 throw off	shuǎi	(动) move back and forth; swing 2 leave sb. behind;

退	tuì	(动) move back; retreat:
绕	rào	(动) move round; circle 2 bypass; go round
往返	Wǎngfǎn	(动) move to and from; go and come back; return
围绕	wéirào	(动) move; round:
博物馆	bówùguǎn	(动) museum:
叙述	xùshù	(动) narrate; recount; relate; account; give an account of; description
必需	bìxū	(动) necessary; indispensable:
否定	fǒudìng	(动) negate; deny
点头	diǎn tóu	(动) nod (as a sign of greeting, approval, etc.):
不如	bùrú	(动) not as good as; inferior to:
培养	péiyǎng	(动) nurture; foster:
服从	fúcóng	(动) obey; be subordinated to:
遵守	zūnshǒu	(动) observe; abide by; adhere to; comply with:
观察	guānchá	(动) observe; examine:
睁	zhēng	(动) open (the eyes):
划船	huáchuán	(动) paddle (or row) a boat; go boating
参与	cānyù	(动) participate in:

及格	jígé	(动) pass a test, examination etc. ; pass; be up to the standard
转告	zhuǎngào	(动) pass on a message (to sb.)
转交	zhuǎnjiāo	(动) pass on; forward
粘贴	zhāntiē	(动) paste; stick:
付款	fùkuǎn	(动) pay a sum of money
关怀	guānhuái	(动) pay serious attention to; be concerned about
说服	shuōfú	(动) persuade; convince; bring round:
捡	jiǎn	(动) pick up; collect; gather:
摘	zhāi	(动) pick; pluck; take off:
存	cún	(动) place sth. for safe keeping; deposit:
逗	dòu	(动) play with; tease; tantalize:
推广	tuīguǎng	(动) popularize; spread; extend
具备	jùbèi	(动) possess; have; be provided with:
浇	jiāo	(动) pour liquid on; sprinkle water on:
称赞	chēng zàn	(动) praise; acclaim; commend
保存	bǎocún	(动) preserve; conserve; keep:
假装	jiǎzhuāng	(动) pretend; feign; simulate; make believe:

预防 against :	yùfáng	(动) prevent; take precautions against; guard
产生	chǎnshēng	(动) produce; engender; bring about; give rise to:
促进	cùjìn	(动) promote ; accelerate:
支	zhī	(动) prop up; support:
抗议	kàngyì	(动) protest
贷款	dàikuǎn	(动) provide a loan; loan; credit (名) a loan
出版	Chūbǎn	(动) publish:
发表	fābiǎo	(动) publish; issue:
拆	chāi	(动) pull down; demolish:
实行 implement:	shíxíng	(动) put into practice (or effect); carry out; practice;
展览	zhǎnlǎn	(动) put on display; exhibit; show:
提问	tíwèn	(动) put questions to; quiz; raise a question
摆	bǎi	(动) put; place; arrange:
吵架	chǎojià	(动) quarrel; have a row
排队	páiduì	(动) queue up; stand in a line
实现	shíxiàn	(动) realize; achieve; bring about:
接待	jiēdài	(动) receive; admit:

推荐	tuījiàn	(动) recommend
缩小	suōxiǎo	(动) reduce; narrow (down) :
改革	gǎigé	(动) reform:
挂号	guàhào	(动) register (at a hospital, etc.)
注册	zhùcè	(动) register:
登记	dēngjì	(动) register; enter one's name:
放松	Fàngsōng	(动) relax; slacken; loosen:
凭	píng	(动) rely on; be based on:
记忆	jìyì	(动) remember; recall:
重复	chóngfù	(动) repeat; duplicate
补充	bǔchōng	(动) replenish; supplement; complement; add:
报告	bàogào	(动) report; make known (名) report; speech; lecture:
责备	zébèi	(动) reproach; blame; censure; take sb. to task:
救	jiù	(动) rescue; save; salvage:
敬爱	jìng'ài	(动) respect and love:
尊敬	zūnjìng	(动) respect; esteem; honor.
恢复	huīfù	(动) resume; renew:

保留	bǎoliú	(动) retain:
退休	tuìxiū	(动) retire
修改	xiūgǎi	(动) revise; modify; amend; alter:
乘	chéng	(动) ride:
冲	chōng	(动) rinse; flush; wash away: 2 charge; rush; dash
统治	tǒngzhì	(动) rule; dominate:
逃	táo	(动) run away; escape; flee
闯	chuǎng	(动) rush; force one's way in or out:
维护	wéihù	(动) safeguard; defend; uphold:
讽刺	fèngcì	(动) satirize
骂	mà	(动) scold; curse; swear:
咨询	zīxún	(动) seek advice; consult:
寻找	xúnzhǎo	(动) seek; look for
追求	zhuīqiú	(动) seek; pursue; go after:
仿佛	fǎngfú	(动) seem; as if
销售	xiāoshòu	(动) sell; market:
问候	wènhòu	(动) send one's respects (or regards) to; extend

greetings to:

派	pài	(动) send; dspatch:
结账	jiézhàng	(动) settle (or square) accounts; balance books; to pay the bill
摇	yáo	(动) shake; wave:
发抖	fādǒu	(动) shiver; shake; tremble:
射击	shèjí	(动) shoot; fire
缩短	suōduǎn	(动) shorten; curtail; cut down:
喊	hǎn	(动) shout; cry out; yell:
嚷	rǎng	(动) shout; yell; make an uproar:
孝顺	xiàoshùn	(动) show filial obedience
显示	xiǎnshì	(动) show; demonstrate; manifest:
签字	qiānzì	(动) sign (one's name)
抢	qiǎng	(动) snatch; grab:
打喷嚏	dǎ pēntì	(动) sneeze
征求	Zhēngqiú	(动) solicit; seek; ask for:
吐	tǔ	(动) spit:
流传	liúchuán	(动) spread; circulate; hand down:
洒	sǎ	(动) sprinkle; spray; spill; shed:

独立	dúlì	(动) stand alone; (形) independent; on one's own:
吃亏	chīkuī	(动) stand to lose; get the worst of it:
踩	cǎi	(动) step on; tread; trample
插	chā	(动) stick in; insert; thrust:
刺激	cìjī	(动) stimulate:
炒	chǎo	(动) stir-fry; fry
阻止	zǔzhǐ	(动) stop; prevent; hold back:
强调	qiángdiào	(动) stress; emphasize
伸	shēn	(动) stretch; extend
争取	zhēngqǔ	(动) strive for; fight for; win over:
预订	yùdìng	(动) subscribe; book; place an order
失眠	shīmián	(动) suffer from insomnia
概括	gàikuò	(动) summarize; generalize:
克服	kèfú	(动) surmount; overcome; conquer:
象征	xiàngzhēng	(动) symbolize; signify (名) symbol; token
综合	zònghé	(动) synthesize; bring into a state of balance:
摄影	shèyǐng	(动) take a photograph; picture; have a picture

taken:

冒险	màoxiǎn	(动) take a risk; take chances:
趁	chèn	(动) take advantage of; avail oneself of:
告别	gàobié	(动) take leave (of)
记录	jìlù	(动) take notes; keep the minutes; record: (名) minutes; notes; record:
形成	xíngchéng	(动) take shape; form
发言	fāyán	(动) take the floor; give a speech
胡说	húshuō	(动) talk nonsense; drivel
撕	sī	(动) tear up; tear to pieces
多亏	duōkuī	(动) thanks to; luckily [indicating that owing to some favorable condition, a misfortune is avoided]:
思考	sīkǎo	(动) think deeply; ponder over; reflect on:
吓	xià	(动) threaten ; intimidate
威胁	wēixié	(动) threaten; menace; imperil:
系领带	kì lǐngdài	(动) tie a tie
系	jì	(动) tie; fasten; do up; button up:
祝福	Zhùfú	(动) to bless (名) Blessing; benediction
珍惜	zhēnxī	(动) to cherish; treasure
设计	shèjì	(动) to design; plan: (名) design; plan

缓解	huǎnjiě	(动) to ease; relief
纪录	jìlù	(动) to record (名) the record
休闲	xiūxián	(动) to take leisure, casual activities or recreation
训练	xùnliàn	(动) train; drill
传递	chuándì	(动) transmit; deliver; transfer:
爱惜	àixī	(动) treasure; cherish
对待	duìdài	(动) treat; approach; handle
企图	qìtú	(动) try; attempt; contrive
拐弯	guǎiwān	(动) turn a corner; turn
忍不住	rěn bù zhù	(动) unable to bear; cannot help (doing sth.):
统一	tǒngyī	(动) unify; unite; integrate:
联合	liánhé	(动) unite; ally
利用	lìyòng	(动) use; utilize; make use of:
运用	yùnyòng	(动) utilize; wield; apply; put to use:
违反	wéifǎn	(动) violate; run counter to:
自愿	zìyuàn	(动) volunteer:
等候	děnghòu	(动) wait; await; expect:
等待	děngdài	(动) walt; await:

挥	huī	(动) wave; wield:
打工	dǎgōng	(动) work for others; be employed:
干活儿	gàn huó er	(动) work; do manual labor
发愁	fāchóu	(动) worry; be anxious
包裹	bāoguǒ	(动) wrap up; bind up (名) bundle; package; parcel:
辞职	cízhí	(动) resign

HSK 6 Verb 动词 dòngcí (1014)

留恋	liúliàn	(动) be reluctant to part (from sb. or with sth.); have a sentimental attachrnent for 2 recall with nostalgia
拣	jiǎn	(动) choose; select; pick out:
染	rǎn	(动) dye (to change the colour)
占有	zhànyǒu	(动) own; possess; have 2 occupy; hold

陷入	xiànrù	(动) sink (or fall) into; land oneself in:
培训	péixùn	(动) train (to prepare someone or yourself for a job, activity, or sport, by learning skills and/or by mental or physical exercise) (名) Training
活该	huógāi	(动) (口) serve sb. right; deserved ; deserved it
撒谎	sāhuǎng	(动) (口) tell a lie; lie
折腾	zhēteng	(动) (口) turn from side to side; toss about
弥漫	mímàn	(动) (air, characteristics, or smells etc.) fill the air; spread all over the place; suffuse; pervade
随身	suíshēn	(动) (carry) on one' s person; (take) with one:
打包	dǎbāo	(动) (in a restaurant) have a doggie bag
心疼	xīnténg	(动) (of children) love dearly 2 feel sorry to see sth. running to waste
发行	fāxíng	(动) (of currency, books, etc.) issue; publish; distribute:
熄灭	xímiè	(动) (of fire) go out; die out
堕落	duòluò	(动) (of mind; behaviour) be corrupted; degenerate
涌现	Yǒngxiàn	(动) (of people and events) emerge in large numbers
悬挂	xuánguà	(动) (of portrait, flag, etc.) hang
潜移默化	qiányímòhuà	(动) (of sb.'s character, thinking, etc.) change imperceptibly

发扬　　　　fāyáng　　　　(动) (of spirit, tradition, etc.) develop; foster (to encourage the development or growth of ideas or feelings); carry on

还原　　　　huányuán　　　　(动) (of things) be restored to the original state or shape

驻扎　　　　zhùzhá　　　　(动) (of troops) be stationed

起伏　　　　qǐfú　　　　(动) (of waves, mountain ranges, etc.) rise and fall

构思　　　　gòusī　　　　(动) (of writers or artists) work out the plot of a story or the composition of a painting

为期　　　　wéiqí　　　　(动) (to be completed) by a definite date:

折　　　　zhé　　　　(动) (口) roll over; turn over; to bend

冲突　　　　chōngtú　　　　(动) (名) conflict; clash

奖励　　　　jiǎnglì　　　　(动) (名) encourage and reward; award; reward:

呻吟　　　　shēnyín　　　　(动) (名) groan (showing great pain or unhappiness); moan (to make a long, low sound of pain, suffering, or another strong emotion)

提示　　　　tíshì　　　　(动) (名) point out; prompt; prompting; presentation, clue; hint

提议　　　　tíyì　　　　(动) (名) propose ; suggest; move

补救　　　　bǔjiù　　　　(动) (名) remedy (to do something to correct or improve something that is wrong)

牺牲　　　　xīshēng　　　　　　(动) (名) sacrifice (to give up something that is valuable to you in order to help another person) (动) lay down one's life, die

罢工　　　　bàgōng　　　　　　(动) (名) strike; go on strike (to refuse to continue working)

不敢当　　　bù gǎndāng　　　　(动) [a polite expression in reply to a compliment] I wish I could deserve your compliment; you flatter me

在乎　　　　zàihū　　　　　　　(动) [often but not always used in the negative] care about; mind; take to heart:

巩固　　　　gǒnggù　　　　　　(动) [often used in figurative sense] consolidate; strengthen; solidify

理睬　　　　lǐcǎi　　　　　　　(动) [often used in negative sentences] pay attention to; show interest in:

意识　　　　yìshí　　　　　　　(动) 1 [often used with 到] be aware of; realize:

　　　　　　　　　　　　　　　(名) 2 consciousness

在意　　　　zàiyì　　　　　　　(动) [usu. used in the negative] care about; mind; take to heart:

支配　　　　zhīpèi　　　　　　(动) 1 allocate; arrange 2 control; determine

辅助　　　　fǔzhù　　　　　　　(动) 1 assist 2 (形) supplementary; subsidiary

忌讳	jìhuì	(动) 1 avoid as taboo: 3 avoid as harmful; abstain from (名) taboo
颁发	bānfā	(动) 1 award 2 issue; promulgate (to announce something publicly, especially a new law)
泛滥	fànlàn	(动) 1 be in flood; overflow 2 spread unchecked
沸腾	fèiténg	(动) 1 boil 2 seethe with excitement
熬	áo	(动) 1 boil; stew 2 endure (pain or hardships)
兑现	duìxiàn	(动) 1 cash (a cheque, etc.) 2 realize; fulfil (promise)
蒙	mēng	(动) 1 cheat; deceive 2 make a random guess
收缩	shōusuō	(动) 1 contract; shrink: 2 concentrate one's forces; draw back
栽培	zāipéi	(动) 1 cultivate; grow 2 foster; train (qualified personnel); educate
示威	shìwēi	(动) 1 demonstrate; hold a demonstration 2 put on a show of force; display one's strength
解散	jiěsàn	(动) 1 dismiss 2 dissolve; disband
划分	huàfēn	(动) 1 divide 2 differentiate
烘	Hōng	(动) 1 dry or warm by the fire 2 set off
跌	diē	(动) 1 fall; tumble:

为难	wéinán	(动) 1 feel embarrassed: 2 make things difficult for:
振奋	zhènfèn	(动) 1 feel invigorated; be filled with enthusiasm 2 inspire; stimulate
哄	hōng	(动) 1 fool; humbug: 2 coax (to persuade someone gently to do something or go somewhere, by being kind and patient); humour (to do what someone wants so that they do not become annoyed or upset)
凑合	còuhé	(动) 1 gather together (形) passable (satisfactory but not excellent)
散发	sànfà	(动) 1 give off; send forth; diffuse; emit 2 distribute; issue; give out
交代	jiāodài	(动) 1 hand over 2 explain; make clear; brief; tell
吊	diào	(动) 1 hang; suspend; 2 revoke; withdraw
立足	lìzú	(动) 1 have a foothold somewhere 2 base oneself upon:
捧	pěng	(动) 1 hold in both hands: 2 extol; flatter
感染	gǎnrǎn	(动) 1 infect 2 influence; affect:
交叉	jiāochā	(动) 1 intersect; cross; crisscross:
踊跃	yǒngyuè	(动) 1 leap; jump 2 (形) eagerly; enthusiastically
放手	fàngshǒu	(动) 1 let go; release one's hold 2 have a free hand
趴	pā	(动) 1 lie on one's stomach; lie prone 2 bend over

探望	tànwàng	(动) 1 look (to pay a visit sb.) : 2 visit
起哄	qǐhòng	(动) 1 make trouble; create disturbance 2 (of a crowd of people) jeer; boo and hoot
调剂	tiáojì	(动) 1 make up (or fill) a prescription 2 adjust; regulate:
制造	zhìzào	(动) 1 make; manufacture 2 create; fabricate:
眯	mī	(动) 1 narrow one's eyes 2 take a nap
埋没	máimò	(动) 1 neglect; stifle (to prevent something from happening, being expressed, or continuing) 2 cover up; bury
出卖	chūmài	(动) 1 offer for sale; sell 2 betray; sell out
操纵	cāozòng	(动) 1 operate; control (动) 2 manipulate
徘徊	páihuái	(动) 1 pace up and down 2 hesitate; waver
砸	zá	(动) 1 pound; tamp 2 break; smash
扒	bā	(动) 1 push aside 2 strip off; take off
搭	dā	(动) 1 put up; build 2 come into contact; join
颠倒	diāndǎo	(动) 1 put upside down; reverse; invert 2 be confused
缓和	huǎnhé	(动) 1 relax; ease up; mitigate ; alleviate 2 calm down
回报	huíbào	(动) 1 report back 2 repay; requite ; reciprocate

申报 (to the Customs)	shēnbào	(动) 1 report; submit to a higher body 2 declare sth.
寄托 place (hope, etc.) on	jìtuō	(动) 1 send to the care of sb. ; leave with sb .2
转移	Zhuǎnyí	(动) 1 shift; transfer 2 divert
溜	liū	(动) 1 slide; glide 2 sneak off ; slip away
铺	pū	(动) 1 spread; extend; unfold: 2 pave; lay
发动	fādòng	(动) 1 start; launch 2 arouse; mobilize:
斗争 (名) struggle	dòuzhēng	(动) 1 struggle; fight; combat 2 strive for; fight for
搀	chān	(动) 1 support or help sb. by the arm
憋 feel oppressed	biē	(动) 1 suppress; hold back; restrain 2 suffocate ;
掀起	xiānqǐ	(动) 1 surge 2 (of movement) set off; start
保养 2 maintain; keep in good repair	bǎoyǎng	(动) 1 take good care of (or conserve) one's health:
策划 meeting, performance etc.)	cèhuà	(动) 1 to plan; plot, scheme 2 to design (party,
动手 hand to strike; hit out	dòngshǒu	(动) 1 touch 2 start work; get to work 3 raise a

调动	diàodòng	(动) 1 transfer; shift:
当心	dāngxīn	(动) look out; take care; be careful:
磕	kē	(动) 2 knock (against sth hard) 2 kowtow
废除	fèichú	(动) abolish; abrogate (law, treaty, rule, etc.)
盛产	shèngchǎn	(动) abound in
摄取	shèqǔ	(动) absorb; assimilate:
留念	liúniàn	(动) accept or keep as a souvenir
验收	yànshōu	(动) accept sth. as up to standard after a check
采纳	cǎinà	(动) accept; adopt
迁就	qiānjiù	(动) accommodate oneself to:
攒	zǎn	(动) accumulate; hoard; save:
充当	chōngdāng	(动) act as; serve as; play the part of
代理	dàilǐ	(动) act on sb.'s behalf; act for: 2 act as agent (or proxy, procura tor) (名) agent; deputy; proxy
统计	tǒngjì	(动) add up; count: (名) statistics:
增添	zēngtiān	(动) add; increase:
治理	zhìlǐ	(动) administer; govern:
钦佩	qīnpèi	(动) admire; esteem:

循序渐进	xún xù jiànjìn	(动) advance by stages
加剧	jiājù	(动) aggravate; intensify; exacerbate:
鼓动	gǔdòng	(动) agitate ; arouse; instigate
力争	lìzhēng	(动) aim high; strive to
惊动	jīngdòng	(动) alarm; alert; bother; disturb:
配备	pèibèi	(动) 1 allocate; provide; equip
		(名) 2 outfit; equipment:
共计	gòngjì	(动) amount to; add up to; total
停泊	tíngbó	(动) anchor a ship; lie at anchor.
意料	yìliào	(动) anticipate; expect:
呼吁	hūyù	(动) appeal (a request to the public for money,

information, or help); call on:

涂抹	túmǒ	(动) apply (to spread or rub a substance such as

cream or paint on a surface)

任命	rènmìng	(动) appoint:
指定	zhǐdìng	(动) appomt; assign; name:
鉴定	jiàndìng	(动) 1 appraise; identify; authenticate; determine

(名) 2 appraisal (of a person's strong and weak points):

审美	shěnměi	(动) appreciate the beauty of:
赞同	zàntóng	(动) approve of; endorse:
认可	rènkě	(动) approve:
激发	jīfā	(动) arouse; stimulate; set off
搭配	dāpèi	(动) arrange (in pairs or group); combine
逮捕	dàibǔ	(动) arrest; take into custody:
降临	jiànglín	(动) arrive; come; befall (If something bad or dangerous

befalls you, it happens to you.)

抵达	dǐdá	(动) arrive; reach
请教	qǐngjiào	(动) ask for advice; consult:
请示	qǐngshì	(动) ask for instructions:
报销	bàoxiāo	(动) ask for reimbursement:
反问	fǎnwèn	(动) ask in retort
评估	pínggū	(动) assess:
协助	xiézhù	(动) assist
联想	liánxiǎng	(动) associate sth. with (in the mind)
交往	jiāowǎng	(动) associate with; make contact with:

就职	jiùzhí	(动) assume office:
担保	dānbǎo	(动) assure; guarantee:
攻击	gōngjí	(动) attack ; assault:
进攻	jìngōng	(动) attack; assault:
袭击	xíjí	(动) attack; raid:
妄想	wàngxiǎng	(动) attempt in vain
		(名) vain hope; wishful thinking
尝试	chángshì	(动) attempt; try
试图	shìtú	(动) attempt; try
报仇	bàochóu	(动) avenge; revenge:
觉醒	juéxǐng	(动) awaken; come to realize the truth; suddenly

see the light; become aware of

取缔	qǔdì	(动) ban; outlaw
讨价还价	tǎojiàhuánjià	(动) bargain; haggle
沐浴	mùyù	(动) bathe; be bathed in
缺席	quēxí	(动) be absent from a meeting，etc.:

上瘾	shàngyǐn	(动) be addicted (to sth.); get into the habit (of doing sth.) :
诞生	dànshēng	(动) be born; come into being; emerge
濒临	bīnlín	(动) be close to; border on; be on the verge of:
服气	fúqì	(动) be convinced:
盛行	shèngxíng	(动) be current (or rife, rampant); be in vogue
确信	quèxìn	(动) be deeply convinced
认定	rèndìng	(动) be deeply convinced; set one's mind on
滞留	zhìliú	(动) be detained; be held up
泄气	xièqì	(动) be discouraged; be dampened
便于	biànyú	(动) be easy to; be convenient for:
当选	dāngxuǎn	(动) be elected
相等	xiāngděng	(动) be equal:
着迷	zháomí	(动) be fascinated; be held spellbound
遍布	biànbù	(动) be found everywhere; spread all over
陷害	xiànhài	(动) be framed (to make a person seem to be guilty of a crime when they are not, by producing facts or information that are not true)
赞叹	zàntàn	(动) be full of praise; be filled with admiration for
擅长	shàncháng	(动) be good at; be expert in; be skilled in:

敌视	díshì	(动) be hostile (or antagonistic) to
主管	zhǔguǎn	(动) be in charge of; be responsible for
调和	tiáohé	(动) be in harmonious proportion 2 mediate;

reconcile: (名) compromise; make concessions

领先	lǐngxiān	(动) be in the lead; lead:
嫉妒	jídù	(动) be jealous of (unhappy and angry because

someone has something that you want); envy (to wish that you had something that another person has)

局限	júxiàn	(动) be limited; confine
位于	wèiyú	(动) be located; be situated; lie:
出神	chūshén	(动) be lost in thought; be spellbound:
沉思	chénsī	(动) be lost in thought; ponder; contemplate
夹杂	jiázá	(动) be mixed up with; be mingled with
观光	guānguāng	(动) be on a sightseeing trip
值班	zhíbān	(动) be on duty
警惕	jǐngtì	(动) be on guard against; watch out for; be vigilant
巴不得	bābudé	(动) be only too glad (to do sth,) ; eagerly look

forward to; earnestly wish:

敷衍	fūyǎn	(动) be perfunctory (done quickly, without taking

care or interest)

孕育	yùnyù	(动) be pregnant with; breed:
怀孕	huáiyùn	(动) be pregnant; conceived:
精通	jīngtōng	(动) be proficient in; well versed in; have a good command of; master:
问世	wèn shì	(动) be published for the first title; come out
勇于	yǒngyú	(动) be ready to; never hesitate to; have the courage to
间隔	jiàngé	(动) be separated from.
诧异	chàyì	(动) be surprised; be astonished
自主	zìzhǔ	(动) be the master of one's own fate: -
甘心	gānxīn	(动) be willing to
乐意	lèyì	(动) be willing to; be ready to:
不愧	bùkuì	(动) be worthy of; deserve to be called; prove oneself to be:
吃苦	chīkǔ	(动) bear hardships:
忍受	rěnshòu	(动) bear; endure
殴打	ōudǎ	(动) beat up; hit:
揍	zòu	(动) beat: hit: strike:
作废	zuòfèi	(动) become in valid:

和解	héjiě	(动) become reconciled (become friendly again after they have argued.)
着手	zhuóshǒu	(动) begin; set about:
信仰	xìnyǎng	(动) believe in (名) faith; belief; conviction:
扑	pū	(动) bend over
沾光	zhānguāng	(动) benefit from one's association with sb. or sth.
包围	bāowéi	(动) besiege (to surround a place, especially with an army); surround; encircle.
赋予	fùyǔ	(动) bestow; endow.
背叛	bèipàn	(动) betray; forsake
苦尽甘来	kǔjìngānlái	(动) bitterness finishes, sweetness begins (idiom); the hard times are over, the good times just beginning
责怪	zéguài	(动) blame:
眨	zhǎ	(动) blink (one's eyes); wink:
封锁	fēngsuǒ	(动) blockade; block; seal off:
盛开	shèngkāi	(动) Bloom; be in full bloom
抹杀	mǒshā	(动) blot out; obliterate
吹牛	chuīniú	(动) boast; brag:
鞠躬	jūgōng	(动) bow:

掰	Bāi	(动) break off with the fingers and thumb:
断绝	duànjué	(动) break off; cut off; sever:
突破	túpò	(动) break through
哺乳	bǔrǔ	(动) breastfeed
呵	hē	(动) breathe out (with the mouth open):
繁殖	fánzhí	(动) breed; reproduce:
酝酿	yùnniàng	(动) brew; ferment:
复活	fùhuó	(动) bring back to life; revive
冤枉	yuānwǎng	(动) bring false charges against sb
审判	shěnpàn	(动) bring to trial; try:
抚养	fǔyǎng	(动) bring up; foster; raise
播放	bōfàng	(动) broadcast
直播	zhíbò	(动) broadcast a radio or TV programme live (名) live radio or TV transmission
修建	xiūjiàn	(动) build; construct
欺负	qīfù	(动) bully; treat sb. highhandedly
迸发	bèngfā	(动) burst forth; burst out :
埋葬	máizàng	(动) bury

不择手段　　　　　　bùzéshǒuduàn　　　　　　(动) by fair means Or foul; by hook or by crook; unscrupulously

看望　　　　kànwàng　　　　(动) call on; visit; see:

做主　　　　zuò zhǔ　　　　(动) Call the shots

没辙　　　　méizhé　　　　(动) can find no way out; be at the end of one' s rope

恨不得　　　　hènbudé　　　　(动) Can not wait

撤销　　　　chèxiāo　　　　(动) cancel; revoke:

不堪　　　　bùkān　　　　(动) cannot bear; Cannot stand:

俘虏　　　　fúlǔ　　　　(动) capture: take prisoner

　　　　　　　　　　(名) captive: prisoner of war (P. O. W.)

占领　　　　zhànlǐng　　　　(动) capture; occupy; seize:

精打细算　　jīngdǎxìsuàn　　(动) careful calculation and strict budgeting; practise economy by meticulous calculation

继往开来　　jìwǎngkāilái　　(动) carry forward the cause of the older generation and break new ground

挎　　　　kuà　　　　(动) carry on the arm:

扛　　　　káng　　　　(动) carry on the shoulder; shoulder:

落实	luòshí	(动) carry out; fulfil; implement; put into effect
贯彻	guànchè	(动) carry through (or out); implement:
雕刻	diāokè	(动) carve; engrave:
铸造	zhùzào	(动) cast
捕捉	bǔzhuō	(动) catch ; seize
轰动	hōngdòng	(动) cause a sensation; make a stir:
折磨	zhémó	(动) cause physical or mental suffering; torment
指责	zhǐzé	(动) censure; criticize :
日新月异	rìxīnyuèyì	(动) change with each passing day; make rapid progress
制止	zhìzhǐ	(动) check; stop; curb:
咀嚼	jǔjué	(动) chew （to crush food into smaller, softer pieces with the teeth so that it can be swallowed）
飞翔	fēixiáng	(动) circle in the air; hover
流通	liútōng	(动) circulate (to go around or through something, like blood in body, currency)
循环	xúnhuán	(动) circulate; cycle:
表彰	biǎozhāng	(动) cite (in dispatches) ; commend
索赔	suǒpéi	(动) claim damages; claim an indemnity

清除	qīngchú	(动) clear away; get rid of; eliminate
攀登	pāndēng	(动) climb; clamber; scale
倒闭	dǎobì	(动) close down; go bankrupt:
怠慢	dàimàn	(动) cold-shoulder (to deliberately ignore someone

in an unfriendly way); slight (to insult someone by ignoring them or treating them as if not important)

崩溃	bēngkuì	(动) collapse; break down; crumble
塌	tā	(动) collapse; fall down; cave in
回收	huíshōu	(动) collect; recycle
收藏	shōucáng	(动) collect; store up:
勾结	gōujié	(动) collude with; conspire with
合并	hébìng	(动) combine:
逢	féng	(动) come across; meet; chance upon:
妥协	tuǒxié	(动) come to terms ; compromise:

觉悟	Juéwù	(动)1 come to understand; become aware of consciousness ;
		(名) awareness; understanding:
评论	pínglùn	(动) comment on:

对照	duìzhào	(动) compare; collate:
补偿	bǔcháng	(动) compensate; make up :
埋怨	mányuàn	(动) complain; grumble; blame
相辅相成	xiāngfǔxiāngchéng	(动) complement each other; be complementary (to each other)
合成	héchéng	(动) compose; compound:
领悟	lǐngwù	(动) comprehend; grasp:
隐瞒	yǐnmán	(动) conceal; hide; hold back:
隐蔽	yǐn bì	(动) conceal; take cover
致力于	zhìlì yú	(动) concentrate on; be devoted to
签订	qiāndìng	(动) conclude and sign (an agreement etc.):
谴责	qiǎnzé	(动) condemn; denounce
凝聚	níngjù	(动) condense:
授予	shòuyǔ	(动) confer; award
证实	zhèngshí	(动) confirm ; verify; bear out:
合乎	héhū	(动) conform with (or to); correspond to; accord with; tally with:
征服	Zhēngfú	(动) conquer; subjugate:
着想	zhuóxiǎng	(动) consider (the interests of sb. or sth.)

斟酌	zhēnzhuó	(动) consider; deliberate (to think or talk seriously and carefully about something)
托运	tuōyùn	(动) consign for shipment; check:
精益求精	jīngyìqiújīng	(动) constantly improve one's skill; keep improving:
协商	xiéshāng	(动) consult; be in consultation with
磋商	cuōshāng	(动) consult; exchange views; hold a discussion
参照	cānzhào	(动) consult; refer to
耗费	hàofèi	(动) consume; expend (to use or spend time, effort, or money)
消耗	xiāohào	(动) consume; use up
压抑	yāyì	(动) contain; inhibit; depress:
延续	yánxù	(动) continue; go on; last:
承包	chéngbāo	(动) contract
垄断	lǒngduàn	(动) control; monopolize:
冷却	lěngquè	(动) cool off:
照应	zhàoyìng	(动) coordinate, correlate
对付	duìfù	(动) cope with.
纠正	jiūzhèng	(动) correct; put right; redress

腐蚀	fǔshí	(动) corrupt; corrode:
算数	suànshù	(动) coun t; hold: stand:
惹祸	rěhuò	(动) court disaster
掩饰	yǎnshì	(动) cover up; gloss over; conceal:
覆盖	fùgài	(动) cover:
掩盖	yǎngài	(动) cover; conceal:
创作	chuàngzuò	(动) create (write literary works): (名) literary and artistic creation
扰乱	rǎoluàn	(动) create confusion; disturb
批判	pīpàn	(动) criticize; repudiate
杂交	zájiāo	(动) cross-breed; hybridize
结晶	jiéjīng	(动) crystallize (名) crystal
培育	péiyù	(动) cultivate; foster; breed:
割	gē	(动) cut
剪彩	jiǎncǎi	(动) cut the ribbon at an opening ceremony
玩弄	wànnòng	(动) dally with sb (to be romantically or sexually involved with someone, usually for a short time, without really loving that person) 2 play with; juggle with

务实 pragmatic:	wùshí	(动) deal with concrete matters relating to work; be
处置	chǔzhì	(动) deal with; handle:
欺骗	qīpiàn	(动) deceive; cheat; dupe; swindle
表决	biǎojué	(动) decide by vote; vote:
悔恨	huǐhèn	(动) deeply regret; be filled with remorse
防守	fángshǒu	(动) defend; guard
捍卫	hànwèi	(动) defend; guard; protect:
保卫	bǎowèi	(动) defend; safeguard:
诈骗	zhàpiàn	(动) defraud; swindle
拖延	tuōyán	(动) delay; put off; procrastinate:
贬低	biǎndī	(动) deliberately underestimate; play down
依赖	yīlài	(动) depend on:
描绘	miáohuì	(动) depict; describe; portray
抛弃	pāoqì	(动) desert; forsake; discard:
蔑视	mièshì	(动) despise; scorn; show contempt for
销毁	xiāohuǐ	(动) destroy by melting or burning:
毁灭	huǐmiè	(动) destroy; exterminate; wipe out

拘留	jūliú	(动) detain; be taken into custody:
振兴	zhènxīng	(动) develop vigorously; promote:
演变	yǎnbiàn	(动) develop; evolve:
开展	kāizhǎn	(动) develop; launch; unfold; promote; carry out
拨打	bōdǎ	(动) dial a telephone number
死亡	sǐwáng	(动) die (名) death
相差	xiāngchà	(动) differ (to be not like something or someone else; the difference between)
失踪	shīzōng	(动) disappear; be missing
创新	chuàngxīn	(动) discard old ideas and bring forth new ones; blaze new trails
排放	páifàng	(动) Discharge (名) Emission
歧视	qíshì	(动) discriminate against:
消毒	xiāodú	(动) disinfect; sterilize
解体	jiětǐ	(动) disintegrate; fall apart:
嫌	xián	(动) dislike
解雇	jiěgù	(动) dismiss; fire; sack
分散	fēnsàn	(动) disperse; scatter; decentralize:
陈列	chénliè	(动) display; exhibit:

解剖	jiěpōu	(动) dissect:
溶解	róngjiě	(动) dissolve.
分辨	fēnbiàn	(动) distinguish; differentiate:
鉴别	jiànbié	(动) distinguish; differentiate; judge:
识别	shìbié	(动) distinguish; discern; spot
歪曲	wāiqū	(动) distort; misrepresent; twist:
干扰	gānrǎo	(动) disturb; interfere; obstruct
甭	béng	(动) don't; needn't (不 + 用)
起草	qǐcǎo	(动) draft; draw up:
捞	lāo	(动) drag for; dredge up; fish for; scoop up from

the water 2 get by improper means; gain

| 拽 | zhuài | (动) drag: |

画蛇添足　huàshétiānzú　　(动) draw a snake and add feet to it-- spoil the show by doing sth. quite superfluous

靠拢	kàolǒng	(动) draw close; close up:
掏	tāo	(动) draw out; pull out:
拟定	nǐdìng	(动) draw up; draft; work out:
吸取	xīqǔ	(动) draw; assimilate:
操练	cāoliàn	(动) drill; practise

驱逐	qūzhú	(动) drive out; expel; banish:
要命	yàomìng	(动) drive sb. to his death; kill
暗示	ànshì	(动) drop a hint; hint:
晾	liàng	(动) dry in the air; dry in the sun:
附和	fùhè	(动) echo; parrot (to repeat exactly what someone else says)
教养	jiàoyǎng	(动) educate and train (the younger generation) 2 (名) moral education; culture breeding:
淘汰	táotài	(动) eliminate through selection or competition; be sifted out; weed out
消除	xiāochú	(动) eliminate; dispel; remove:
点缀	diǎnzhuì	(动) embellish; adorn
绣	xiù	(动) embroider
激励	jīlì	(动) encourage; impel; urge
勉励	miǎnlì	(动) encourage; urge
受罪	shòuzuì	(动) endure hardships or tortures; have a hard time
打架	dǎjià	(动) engage in a brawl; come to blows; fight
考古	kǎogǔ	(动) engage in archaeological studies
应酬	yìngchóu	(动) engage in social activities 2 (名) dinner party:

放大	fàngdà	(动) enlarge; magnify; amplify:
肥田	féitián	(动) enrich the soil
保障	bǎozhàng	(动) ensure; guarantee; safeguard:
确保	quèbǎo	(动) ensure; guarantee:
竞选	jìngxuǎn	(动) enter into an election contest; campaign for (office); run for:
诱惑	yòuhuò	(动) entice; tempt; seduce; lure
列举	lièjǔ	(动) enumerate; list:
笼罩	lóngzhào	(动) envelop; shroud
装备	zhuāngbèi	(动) equip; furnish; fit out (名) equipment; installation
爆发	bàofā	(动) erupt; burst out; break out:
确立	quèlì	(动) establish
奠定	diàndìng	(动) establish (a foundation）; settle
设立	shèlì	(动) establish: set up: found:
回避	huíbì	(动) evade; dodge; avoid (meeting sb.):
蒸发	zhēngfā	(动) evaporate
各抒己见	gèshūjǐjiàn	(动) everybody may air his views.
考核	kǎohé	(动) examine; check; assess (sb.'s proficiency):

审查	shěnchá	(动) examme; investigate:
挖掘	wājué	(动) excavate ; unearth:
寒暄	hánxuān	(动) exchange greetings
兑换	duìhuàn	(动) exchange; convert:
忍耐	rěnnài	(动) exercise patience; restrain oneself
熏陶	xūntáo	(动) exert a gradual, uplifting influence on; nurture;

edify (to improve someone's mind)

施加	shījiā	(动) exert; bring to bear on:
并存	bìngcún	(动) exist side by side; coexist
扩张	kuòzhāng	(动) expand; enlarge; extend; spread:
扩充	kuòchōng	(动) expand; strengthen; augment:
预期	yùqí	(动) expect; anticipate :
预料	yùliào	(动) expect; predict; anticipate
开除	kāichú	(动) expel; discharge:
爆炸	bàozhà	(动) explode; blow up; detonate
剥削	bōxuē	(动) exploit (名) exploitation
探索	tànsuǒ	(动) explore; probe:
勘探	kāntàn	(动) explore; prospect (to search for gold, oil, or

other valuable substances on or under the surface of the earth)

暴露	bàolù	(动) expose; reveal; lay bare:
揭露	jiēlù	(动) expose; uncover; bring to light:
揭发	jiēfā	(动) expose; unmask; bring to light
阐述	chǎnshù	(动) expound; elaborate; set forth:
慰问	wèiwèn	(动) express sympathy and solicitude for:
延伸	yánshēn	(动) extend; stretch:
提炼	tíliàn	(动) extract; refine
辜负	Gūfù	(动) fail to live up to; disappoint; let down; be

unworthy of

衰退	shuāituì	(动) fail; decline
瓦解	wǎjiě	(动) fall apart; collapse; crumble
巴结	bājié	(动) fawn on; curry favour with:
恐惧	kǒngjù	(动) fear; dread
畏惧	wèijù	(动) fear; dread:
纳闷儿	nàmèn er	(动) feel puzzled; be perplexed; wonder:
惋惜	wànxí	(动) feel regret at sth. ; condole with sb. over sth.

unfortunate

恶心	ěxīn	(动) 1. feel sick; feel nauseated
		2 (形) disgusting; revolting

疑惑	yíhuò	(动) feel uncertain ; not be convinced:
争夺	zhēngduó	(动) fight (or contend, scramble) for; vie with sb. for sth.: -
打仗	dǎzhàng	(动) fight a battle.
战斗	zhàndòu	(动) fight; combat: (名) battle; action:
过滤	guòlǜ	(动) filter; infiltrate:
安置	ānzhì	(动) find a place for; help settle down; arrange for:
发觉	fājué	(动) find; realize; discover
完毕	wánbì	(动) finish; complete; end, be ready
布置	bùzhì	(动) fix up; arrange; decorate:
吹捧	chuīpěng	(动) flatter; lavish praise on:
窜	cuàn	(动) flee; scurry:
漂浮	piāofú	(动) float (形) (of style of work) superficial; showy
跟随	Gēnsuí	(动) follow:
遵循	zūnxún	(动) follow; adhere to (principle, political line, etc.)
譬如	pìrú	(动) for example

勉强　　　　　miǎnqiáng　　　　(动) force sb. to do sth. (形) 1 do one' s best despite difficulty or lack of experience 2 reluctantly; grudgingly 3 inadequate; unconvincing; far fetched 4 barely enough

强制　　　　　qiángzhì　　　　　(动) force; compel (by political or economic means):

强迫　　　　　qiǎngpò　　　　　(动) force; compel; coerce

逼迫　　　　　bīpò　　　　　　　(动) force; compel; pressurize

伪造　　　　　wèizào　　　　　　(动) forge; falsify; fabricate; counterfeit:

算了　　　　　suànle　　　　　　(动) forget it; let it pass:

饶恕　　　　　ráoshù　　　　　　(动) forgive; pardon

配套　　　　　pèitào　　　　　　(动) form a complete set:

断定　　　　　duàndìng　　　　　(动) form a judgment; conclude

合伙　　　　　héhuǒ　　　　　　(动) form a partnership:

制订　　　　　zhìdìng　　　　　　(动) formulate; work out

创立　　　　　chuànglì　　　　　(动) found; originate

诬陷　　　　　wúxiàn　　　　　　(动) frame a case against sb.

冻结　　　　　dòngjié　　　　　　(动) freeze:

采集　　　　　cǎijí　　　　　　　(动) gather; collect:

盯　　　　　　dīng　　　　　　　(动) gaze at; stare at; fix one's eyes on:

凝视	níngshì	(动) gaze fixedly; stare
公认	gōngrèn	(动) generally recognize; universally acknowledge
发火	fāhuǒ	(动) get angry; flare up; lose one's temper
挨	āi	(动) get close to; be next or near to
冲动	chōngdòng	(动) get excited; be impetuous (名) impulse
联络	liánluò	(动) get in touch with (名) contact; liaison:
发财	fācái	(动) get rich; make a good deal of money
摆脱	bǎituō	(动) get rid of (restraint, difficulty, or any other undesirable state of things):
排除	páichú	(动) get rid of; remove; elimmate:
生锈	shēng xiù	(动) get rusty
演讲	yǎnjiǎng	(动) give a lecture; make a speech
演奏	yǎnzòu	(动) give an instrumental performance; play a musical instrument (in a performance)
归还	guīhuán	(动) give back; return
生育	shēngyù	(动) give birth to; bear:
资助	zīzhù	(动) give financial aid
赠送	zèngsòng	(动) give sth. to sb. as a gift; handsel; to present
绝望	juéwàng	(动) give up all hope; despair:

| 予以 | yǔyǐ | (动) give; grant: |
| 咬牙切齿 | yǎoyáqièchǐ | (动) gnash one's teeth (when you are angry) |

啃　　　　kěn　　　　(动) gnaw (to bite or chew something repeatedly); nibble (to eat something by taking a lot of small bites) 2 take great pains with one's studies

变质　　　biànzhì　　　(动) go bad; be intrinsically changed for the worse; degenerate (to become worse in quality)

打猎	dǎliè	(动) go hunting
经商	jīngshāng	(动) go into business
生效	shēngxiào	(动) go into effect; become effective:
打官司	dǎ guānsī	(动) go to law
潜水	qiánshuǐ	(动) go under water; dive:
摸索	mōsuǒ	(动) grope ; feel about; fumble:

与日俱增　　yǔrìjùzēng　　(动) grow with each passing day; be steady on the increase

滋长　　　zīzhǎng　　　(动) grow; develop [to (cause something to) grow or change into a more advanced, larger, or stronger form]

把关	bǎguān	(动) guard a pass 2 check on
守护	shǒuhù	(动) guard; defend
保守	bǎoshǒu	(动) guard; keep (形) 2 conservative:

戒备	jièbèi	(动) guard; take precautions; be on the alert:
导向	dǎoxiàng	(动) Guide; direct
引导	yǐndǎo	(动) guide; lead :
计较	jìjiào	(动) haggle over; fuss about 2 argue; dispute
较量	jiàoliàng	(动) have a contest; have a trial of strength
联欢	liánhuān	(动) have a get-together (or a party)
团圆	tuányuán	(动) have a reunion
管辖	guǎnxiá	(动) have control over:
周转	zhōuzhuǎn	(动) have enough to meet the need: (名) turnover (of capital, fund, cash etc.)
饱经沧桑	bǎojīngcāngsāng	(动) have experienced many vicissitudes of life
借助	jièzhù	(动) have the aid of; draw support from:
迟疑	chíyí	(动) hesitate:
踌躇	chóuchú	(动) hesitate; shilly-shally:
阻碍	zǔ'ài	(动) hinder; impede:
打击	dǎjí	(动) hit; strike; attack
捏	niē	(动) hold between the fingers ; pinch:
搂	lǒu	(动) hold in one's arms; hug; embrace

蕴藏	yùncáng	(动) hold in store; contain:
叼	diāo	(动) hold in the mouth
容纳	róngnà	(动) hold; have a capacity of:
梦想	mèngxiǎng	(动) hope in vain; have a fond dream of (名) fond dream
期望	qīwàng	(动) hope; expect; count on
查获	cháhuò	(动) hunt down and seize; ferret out; track down
辨认	biànrèn	(动) identify; recognize
设想	shèxiǎng	(动) imagine; envisage; conceive; assume:
实施	shíshī	(动) implement (to start using a plan or system)
改良	gǎiliáng	(动) improve; ameliorate (to make a bad or unpleasant situation better); reform
不顾	bùgù	(动) in spite of; regardless of:
递增	dìzēng	(动) increase progressively; increase by degrees
指示	zhǐshì	(动) indicate; point out:
推测	tuīcè	(动) infer; conjecture; guess
继承	jìchéng	(动) inherit; carry on:
倡导	chàngdǎo	(动) initiate; propose

注射	zhùshè	(动) inject (to use a needle and syringe (= small tube) to put a liquid such as a drug into a person's body)
镶嵌	xiāngqiàn	(动) inlay; set
挑拨	tiǎobō	(动) instigate; incite:
侮辱	wǔrǔ	(动) insult; humiliate; subject sb. to indignities
干涉	gānshè	(动) interfere; intervene; meddle:
干预	gānyù	(动) intervene ; meddle
侵犯	qīnfàn	(动) intrude; encroach upon; violate:
招投标	zhāo tóubiāo	(动) invite and enter a bid
牵扯	qiānchě	(动) involve; drag in:
涉及	shèjí	(动) involve; relate to; touch upon:
熨	yùn	(动) iron; press
灌溉	guàngài	(动) irrigate
颁布	bānbù	(动) issue; publish; promulgate (to announce something publicly, especially a new law)
发布	fābù	(动) issue; release:
据悉	jùxī	(动) it is reported
衔接	xiánjiē	(动) join; dovetail
颠簸	diānbǒ	(动) jolt; bump; toss:

跳跃	tiàoyuè	(动) jump; leap; bound
犹如	yóurú	(动) just as; like; as if
隔离	gélí	(动) keep apart; isolate:
维修	wéixiū	(动) keep in (good) repair; service; maintain:
惦记	diànjì	(动) keep thinking about
监视	jiānshì	(动) keep watch on; keep an eye on
约束	yuēshù	(动) keep within bounds; restrain; bind:
维持	wéichí	(动) keep; maintain; preserve:
绑架	bǎngjià	(动) kidnap sb
跪	guì	(动) kneel (to go down into, or stay in, a position where one or both knees are on the ground); go down on one's knees
登陆	dēnglù	(动) land; disembark (from a ship)
冲击	chōngjí	(动) lash; pound (名) Impact
嘲笑	cháoxiào	(动) laugh at; ridicule
发射	fāshè	(动) launch ; project ; discharge; fire:
出洋相	chūyángxiàng	(动) lay oneself to ridicule; make a spectacle of oneself
注重	zhùzhòng	(动) lay stress on; emphasize
带领	Dàilǐng	(动) lead; guide

率领	shuàilǐng	(动) lead; head; command:
走漏	zǒulòu	(动) leak out; divulge
泄漏	xièlòu	(动) leak; let out :
拄	zhǔ	(动) lean on (a stick, etc.)
飞跃	fēiyuè	(动) leap:
蹦	bèng	(动) leap; jump; spring:
遗留	yíliú	(动) leave over; hand down:
征收	Zhēngshōu	(动) levy; collect; impose:
舔	tiǎn	(动) lick
埋伏	máifú	(动) lie in ambush; set an ambush; ambush (名) ambush:
倾听	qīngtīng	(动) listen attentively to:
安居乐业	ānjūlèyè	(动) live in peace and work contentedly
居住	jūzhù	(动) live; reside; dwell:
装卸	zhuāngxiè	(动) load and unload
厌恶	yànwù	(动) loathe (to hate someone or something); be disgusted with
登录	dēnglù	(动) log in; sign on
关照	guānzhào	(动) look after; keep an eye on:

东张西望   dōngzhāngxīwàng (动) look around

瞻仰   zhānyǎng   (动) look at with reverence (to sb.'s remains)

注视   zhùshì   (动) look attentively at; gaze at (to look at
something or someone for a long time, especially in surprise or admiration)

回顾   huígù   (动) look back; review

愣   lèng   (动) look distracted; be stupefied:

指望   zhǐwàng   (动) look forward to; count on; expect:

展望   zhǎnwàng   (动) look into the distance:

追究   zhuījiù   (动) look into; get to the roots of (a matter, etc.):

看待   kàndài   (动) look upon; regard; treat

遗失   yíshī   (动) lose

迷失   míshī   (动) lose (one's way, etc.):

丧失   sàngshī   (动) lose; forfeit:

爱戴   àidài   (动) love and esteem (to respect someone or have a
good opinion of them)

保密   bǎomì   (动) maintain secrecy; keep sth. secret:

钻研   zuānyán   (动) mak e a persistent effort to learn.

狠心   hěnxīn   (动) make a determined effort 1 (形) cruel-hearted;
heartless; merciless

致辞	zhìcí	(动) make a speech
体谅	tǐliàng	(动) make allowances for; show understanding and sympathy for; be considerate of sb
破例	pòlì	(动) make an exception
探讨	tàntǎo	(动) make an inquiry into:
洽谈	qiàtán	(动) make arrangements with; talk over with
让步	ràngbù	(动) make concessions; give in; give way; compromise; yield:
更正	gēngzhèng	(动) make corrections (of errors m statements or newspaper articles)
辩解	biànjiě	(动) make excuses
表态	biǎotài	(动) make known one's position
统筹兼顾	tǒngchóu jiāngù	(动) make overall plans and take all factors into consideration
再接再厉	zàijiēzàilì	(动) make persistent efforts; persevere
决策	juécè	(动) make policy; make a strategic decision: (名) policy decision; decision of strategic importance:
进展	jìnzhǎn	(动) make progress; make headway:
报复	bàofù	(动) make reprisal ; retaliate:
捣乱	dǎoluàn	(动) make trouble; create a disturbance

弥补	míbǔ	(动) make up; remedy; make good:
虐待	nüèdài	(动) maltreat; ill-treat
抽空	chōukòng	(动) manage to find time
意味着	yìwèi zhe	(动) mean; imply
打量	dǎliang	(动) measure with the eye; size up:
调解	tiáojiě	(动) mediate; make peace:

遭遇　　　zāoyù　　　(动) meet with; encounter: (名) (bitter) experiencc; (hard) lot:

遭遇许多挫折	zāoyù xǔduō cuòzhé	meet with many setbacks
不幸的遭遇	bùxìng de zāoyù	unfortunate experience
童年的遭遇	tóngnián de zāoyù	one's unhappy childhood experience

遭罪　　　zāozuì　　　(动) endure hardships, tortures, rough conditions, etc.; have a hard time

会晤	huìwù	(动) meet:
磨合	móhé	(动) mesh; work to fit together suitably; rub along together

开采	kāicǎi	(动) mine; extract; exploit:
误解	wùjiě	(动) misread; misunderstand
混合	hùnhé	(动) mix; blend; mingle:
动员	dòngyuán	(动) mobilize; arouse
塑造	sùzào	(动) model; mould
兼职	jiānzhí	(动) moonlight; hold two or more posts concurrently:
追悼	zhuīdào	(动) mourn sb.'s death:
迁徙	qiānxǐ	(动) move to another place; migrate
运行	yùnxíng	(动) move; be in motion:
挪	nuó	(动) move; shift
唠叨	láo dāo	(动) nag (to criticize or complain often in an annoying way)
航行	hángxíng	(动) navigate by water; sail:
忽略	hūlüè	(动) neglect; overlook; lose sight of:
交涉	jiāoshè	(动) negotiate; make representations:
见义勇为	jiànyìyǒngwéi	(动) never hesitate to fight for justice
无可奉告	wú kě fènggào	(动) No comment.
不止	bùzhǐ	(动) not Just ; More than

混淆	hùnxiáo	(动) obscure; blur; confuse; mix up:
阻挠	zǔnáo	(动) obstruct; stand in the way
就业	jiùyè	(动) obtain employment; take up an occupation; get a job:
占据	zhànjù	(动) occupy; hold:
得罪	dézuì	(动) offend
触犯	chùfàn	(动) offend; violate:
奉献	fèngxiàn	(动) offer as a tribute; present with all respect
留神	liúshén	(动) on the alert; take care:
瞪	dèng	(动) open one's eyes wide; stare; glare
开拓	kāità	(动) open up (new area, market); (to do something new and clever, despite any risks)
展示	Zhǎnshì	(动) open up before one's eyes; reveal; show; lay bare:
开辟	kāipì	(动) open up; start:
敞开	chǎngkāi	(动) open wide:
操作	cāozuò	(动) operate (a machine)
压迫	yāpò	(动) oppress; repress 2 constrict
起源	qǐyuán	(动) originate; stem from (名) origin:

急于求成　jí yú qiú chéng　(动) overanxious for quick results; impatient for success

攻克　gōngkè　(动) overcome; capture

重叠　chóngdié　(动) overlap:

过奖　guòjiǎng　(动) overpromise; pay undeserved compliments to:

推翻　tuīfān　(动) overthrow; overturn; topple

包装　bāozhuāng　(动) 1. packing; package (1 to put goods into boxes or containers to be sold; 2 to show someone or something in a particular, usually attractive, way (名) pack; package:

喘气　chuǎnqì　(动) pant (to breathe quickly and loudly); gasp (to take a short, quick breath)

分手　fēnshǒu　(动) part company; say goodbye

逝世　shìshì　(动) pass away

传授　chuánshòu　(动) pass on (knowledge, skill, etc.); impart

转达　zhuǎndá　(动) pass on; convey (one's messsage)

传达　chuándá　(动) pass on; relay:

穿越　chuānyuè　(动) pass through; cut across

巡逻　xúnluó　(动) patrol; (especially of soldiers or the police) to go around an area or a building to see if there is any trouble or danger

开支	kāizhī	(动) pay (expenses); defray (名) expenses; expenditure; spending
拜访	bàifǎng	(动) pay a visit; pay a call on:
偿还	chánghuán	(动) pay back:
支出	zhīchū	(动) pay; expend; disburse 2 (名) expenses; expenditure; outlay
贩卖	fànmài	(动) peddle; traffic; sell:
百分点	bǎifēndiǎn	(动) percentage; Percentage point
履行	lǚxíng	(动) perform; fulfil; carry out:
灭亡	mièwáng	(动) perish; die out; be doomed:
渗透	shèntòu	(动) permeate; seep
许可	xǔkě	(动) permit; allow
迫害	pòhài	(动) persecute :
挑剔	tiāotì	(动) pick holes in; find fault with
拾	shí	(动) pick up (from the ground); collect:
堆积	duījī	(动) pile up; heap up
牵制	qiānzhì	(动) pin down; tie up
掐	qiā	(动) pinch; nip:

俯仰	fǔyǎng	(动) pitch; pitching; tilt; a bending or lifting of the head
耍	shuǎ	(动) play 2 play (tricks)
扮演	bànyǎn	(动) play the part of; act
耕地	gēngdì	(动) plough (名) arable land (Arable farming land is used for, or is suitable for, growing crops)
掠夺	lüèduó	(动) plunder (to steal goods violently from a place, especially during a war); rob (to take money or property illegally from a place, organization, or person, often using violence); pillage (to steal something from a place or a person by using violence, especially during war)
普及	pǔjí	(动) popularize; disseminate; spread
拥有	yǒngyǒu	(动) possess; have; own:
延期	yánqí	(动) postpone; defer; put off:
淋	Lín	(动) pour; drench
作弊	zuòbì	(动) practice fraud; cheat
演习	yǎnxí	(动) practice with live ammunition
倾向	qīngxiàng	(动) prefer (名) trend; tendency
筹备	chóubèi	(动) prepare; arrange
呈现	chéngxiàn	(动) present (a certain appearance); appear; emerge :

压榨 white	yāzhà	(动) press; squeeze 2 exploit; fleece ; bleed sb.
冒充	màochōng	(动) pretend to be; pass oneself off as:
防治	fángzhì	(动) prevent and cure (illness)
防止	fángzhǐ	(动) prevent; guard against; avoid
印刷	yìnshuā	(动) print:
承诺	chéngnuò	(动) promise to undertake
提拔	tíbá	(动) promote (a talent); to raise someone to a higher or more important position or rank
推销	tuīxiāo	(动) promote sales
晋升	jìnshēng	(动) promote to a higher office
支撑	zhīchēng	(动) prop up; shore up; sustain:
宣扬	xuānyáng	(动) propagate; advocate:
预言 prediction:	yùyán	(动) prophesy; predict; foretell (名) prophecy;
挑衅	Tiǎoxìn	(动) provoke an incident
刊登	kāndēng	(动) publish in a newspaper or magazine; carry
惩罚	chéngfá	(动) punish; penalize
采购	cǎigòu	(动) purchase:

争先恐后	zhēngxiānkǒnghòu	(动) push ahead for fear of lagging behind
搁	gē	(动) put side; shelve (to not take action on something until a later time)
记载	jìzǎi	(动) put down in writing; record (名) record; account
清理	qīnglǐ	(动) put in order
化妆	huàzhuāng	(动) put on make-up; make up:
刹车	shāchē	(动) put on the brakes (名) （car) brake
垫	diàn	(动) put sth. under sth. else to raise it or make it level; pad (名) pad; cushion; mat:
盖章	gài zhāng	(动) put the chop (a seal) on
施展	shīzhǎn	(动) put to good use; give free play to:
迷惑	míhuò	(动) puzzle; confuse; perplex; baffle:
引用	yǐnyòng	(动) quote; cite
放射	fàngshè	(动) radiate:
翘	qiào	(动) raise (one's head) 2 stick up; rise on one end; tilt
畜牧	xùmù	(动) raise livestock or poultry:
饲养	sìyǎng	(动) raise; rear:

判决	pànjué	(动) reach a verdict; pass judgment:
达成	dáchéng	(动) reach; conclude:
朗读	lǎngdú	(动) read aloud; read loudly and clearly
背诵	bèisòng	(动) recite from memory
倡议	chàngyì	(动) recommend; propose:
愈	yù	(动) recover; become well 2 (副) [the more the

more . . .] : (same as 越(来越...))

招收	zhāoshōu	(动) recruit; take in:
整顿	zhěngdùn	(动) rectify; consolidate; reorganize:
裁员	cáiyuán	(动) reduce (or dismiss) the staff
压缩	yāsuō	(动) reduce; cut down; curtail:

| 反射 | fǎnshè | (动) reflect (light, heat, sound, or an image) |

(名) reflection; reflex (a physical reaction to

something that you cannot control）

| 谢绝 | xièjué | (动) refuse politely; decline: |

反驳   fǎnbó   (动) refute (to say or prove that a person, statement, opinion, etc. is wrong or false); retort (to answer someone quickly in an angry or funny way 反驳，回嘴); rebut (to argue that a statement or claim is not true)

苏醒   sūxǐng   (动) regain consciousness; come to:

调节   tiáojié   (动) regulate; adjust:

释放   shìfàng   (动) release; set free

救济   jiùjì   (动) relieve; succour:

依靠   yīkào   (动) rely on:

依托   yītuō   (动) Relying on; Relying

遥控   yáokòng   (动) remote control; telecontrol

解除   jiěchú   (动) remove; relieve; get rid of:

租赁   zūlìn   (动) rent; lease; hire

修理   xiūlǐ   (动) repair; mend

修复   xiūfù   (动) repair; restore; renovate

崇敬   chóngjìng   (动) repect; revere:

排斥   páichì   (动) repel; exclude; reject:

更新   gēngxīn   (动) replace; renew; update:

答复   dáfù   (动) reply (formally)

答辩	dábiàn	(动) reply (to a charge, query or an argument):
报到	bàodào	(动) report for work; check in; register:
汇报	huìbào	(动) report; give an account of:
拜托	bàituō	(动) request sb. to do sth. :
抢救	qiǎngjiù	(动) rescue:
挽救	wǎnjiù	(动) rescue; save
抵制	dǐzhì	(动) resist; boycott
对抗	duìkàng	(动) resist; oppose (名) confrontation
反抗	fǎnkàng	(动) resist; revolt:
抵抗	dǐkàng	(动) resist; stand up to:
分解	fēnjiě	(动) resolve; decompose; break down
响应 etc.)	xiǎngyìng	(动) respond; answer (the call of the government,
遏制	èzhì	(动) restrain; contain; keep within limits
抑制	yìzhì	(动) restrain; control
拘束	jūshù	(动) restrain; restrict
制约	zhìyuē	(动) restrict; restrain:
撤退	chètuì	(动) retreat.

精简	jīngjiǎn	(动) retrench; simplify; cut; reduce:
挽回	wǎnhuí	(动) retrieve; redeem:
流露	liúlù	(动) reveal; betray; show unintentionally
复兴	fùxīng	(动) revive（to come or bring something back to life, health, existence, or use）
起义	qǐyì	(动) revolt; rise up (against) 2 (名) uprising
旋转	xuánzhuǎn	(动) revolve; rotate ; spin
讥笑	jīxiào	(动) ridicule; sneer at
造反	zàofǎn	(动) rise in rebellion; rebel; revolt
高涨	gāozhàng	(动) rise; upsurge
拼命	pīnmìng	(动) risk one's life; be reckless
流浪	liúlàng	(动) roam about; lead a vagrant life:
吼	hǒu	(动) roar; howl;
抢劫	qiǎngjié	(动) rob; loot; plunder
摇晃	yáohuàng	(动) rock; sway; shake :
揉	róu	(动) rub (to press or be pressed against something with a circular or up-and-down repeated movement)
摩擦	mócā	(动) rub (名) 1 friction: 2 clash
搓	cuō	(动) rub with the hands

败坏	bàihuài	(动) ruin; undermine:
奔驰	bēnchí	(动) run fast; speed
奔波	bēnbō	(动) rush about; hurry back and forth; be busy

running about; be on the go:

敬礼	jìnglǐ	(动) salute; give a salute
制裁	zhìcái	(动) sanction; punish:
储蓄	chǔ xù	(动) save; deposit:
不屑一顾	bùxiè yī gù	(动) scorn to take a look
掩护	yǎnhù	(动) screen; shield; cover:
封闭	fēngbì	(动) seal off, seal up 2 close down:
密封	mìfēng	(动) seal up:
搜索	sōusuǒ	(动) search for; hunt for; hunt down:
分泌	fēnmì	(动) secrete
沉淀	chéndiàn	(动) sediment; precipitate:
目睹	mùdǔ	(动) see with one's own eyes; witness
实事求是	shíshìqiúshì	(动) seek truth from the facts; be down-to-earth:
寻觅	xúnmì	(动) seek; look for
谋求	móuqiú	(动) seek; strive for:

选拔	xuǎnbá	(动) select (from candidates)
筛选	shāixuǎn	(动) select; choose
自力更生	zìlìgēngshēng	(动) self-reliance; rely on one's own effort
畅销	chàngxiāo	(动) sell well; sell like hot cakes
派遣	pàiqiǎn	(动) send; dispatch:
脱离	tuōlí	(动) separate oneself from; break away from; be divorced from:
示范	shìfàn	(动) set an example; demonstrate:
动身	dòngshēn	(动) set out on a journey; leave
启程	qǐchéng	(动) set out; start on a Journey
树立	shùlì	(动) set up; establish:
设置	shèzhì	(动) set up; put up:
结算	jiésuàn	(动) settle accounts; close an account; make settlement
涮火锅	shuàn huǒguō	(动) Shabu-shabu; Hot Pot
颤抖	Chàndǒu	(动) shake; tremble; quiver; shiver:
分红	fēnhóng	(动) share out profits; pay dividend
遮挡	zhēdǎng	(动) shelter oneself from, keep out:

包庇	bāobì	(动) shield (evildoers and cover up their evil deeds); harbor; cover up :
照耀	zhàoyào	(动) shine, illuminate
震惊	zhènjīng	(动) shock; amaze; astonish:
感慨	gǎnkǎi	(动) sigh with deep feeling
叹气	tànqì	(动) sigh; heave a sigh
签署	qiānshǔ	(动) sign (an aggreement, order, law, etc.)
示意	shìyì	(动) signal; hint; gesture
简化	jiǎnhuà	(动) simplify:
歌颂	gēsòng	(动) sing the praises of; extol; eulogize
旷课	kuàngkè	(动) skip school; play truant
诽谤	fěibàng	(动) slander
诬蔑	wúmiè	(动) slander; vilify:
宰	Zǎi	(动) slaughter; butcher:
粉碎	fěnsuì	(动) smash; shatter; crush 2 broken to pleces
走私	zǒusī	(动) smuggle
爱不释手	Àibùshìshǒu	(动) so delighted with sth, that one can scarcely take one's eyes off it
浸泡	jìnpào	(动) soak

飙升	biāoshēng	(动) soar (to rise very quickly to a high level)
凝固	nínggù	(动) solidify:
播种	bōzhòng	(动) sow seeds:
辩护	biànhù	(动) speak in defence of; try to justify or defend:
赞扬	zànyáng	(动) speak in glowing terms of; pay tribute to
投机	tóujī	(动) speculate (to buy and sell in the hope that the

value of what you buy will increase and that it can then be sold at a higher price in order to make a profit) (名) speculation

挥霍	huīhuò	(动) spend freely; squander
盘旋	pánxuán	(动) spiral; circle
溅	jiàn	(动) splash; spatter (to drop small drops of liquid,

etc. on a surface, or (of liquid) to fall, especially noisily, in small drops)

分裂	fēnliè	(动) split; break up:
劈	pī	(动) split; chop; cleave:
主办	zhǔbàn	(动) sponsor:
扩散	kuòsàn	(动) spread; diffuse:
散布	sànbù	(动) spread; disseminate; scatter; diffuse:
蔓延	mànyán	(动) spread; extend:

泼 pō (动) sprinkle (to drop a few pieces or drops of something over a surface); splash (If a liquid splashes or if you splash a liquid, it falls on or hits something or someone.); spill [to (cause to) flow, move, fall, or spread over the edge or outside the limits of something]

萌芽 méngyá (动) sprout; shoot; bud

鞭策 biāncè (动) spur on; urge on; encourage:

停滞 tíngzhì (动) stagnate; be at a standstill :

并列 bìngliè (动) stand side by side:

高耸 gāosǒng (动) stand tall and erect; tower

高耸 gāosǒng (动) stand tall and erect; tower:

做东 zuò dōng (动) stand treat; play the host

发呆 fādāi (动) stare blankly

创业 chuàngyè (动) start an undertaking; do pioneering work:

陈述 chénshù (动) state (to say or write something, especially clearly and carefully), like state one's views; make one's suggestions.

声明 Shēngmíng (动) state; declare; announce:

盗窃 dàoqiè (动) steal

迈 mài (动) step; stride :

跨 kuà (动) step; stride: 2 bestride; straddle:

不惜	bùxī	(动) stint no effort; not spare :
搅拌	jiǎobàn	(动) stir; mix:
中止	zhōngzhǐ	(动) stop halfway; suspend.
堵塞	dǔsè	(动) stop up; block up:
阻拦	zǔlán	(动) stop; bar the way:
停顿	tíngdùn	(动) stop; halt; pause:
杜绝	dùjué	(动) stop; prevent; put an end to:
储存	chǔcún	(动) store; put away:
储备	chǔbèi	(动) store; reserve; put by (名) reserve
健全	jiànquán	(动) strengthen; amplify; perfect (形) sound; perfect:
着重	zhuózhòng	(动) stress; emphasize:
严禁	yánjìn	(动) strictly forbid (or prohibit)
成交	chéngjiāo	(动) strike a bargain; conclude a transaction ; clinch a deal:
拼搏	pīnbó	(动) struggle hard; exert oneself to the utmost; go all out:
挣扎	zhēngzhá	(动) struggle:
淹没	Yānmò	(动) submerge

屈服	qūfú	(动) submit; yield; bow to:
生存	shēngcún	(动) subsist; exist; live:
充实	chōngshí	(动) substantiate; enrich (形) substantial; rich:
恍然大悟	huǎngrándàwù	(动) suddenly realize; suddenly see the light
遭殃	zāoyāng	(动) suffer disaster or calamity
瘫痪	tānhuàn	(动) suffer from paralysis 2 be paralysed; break down:
遭受	zāoshòu	(动) suffer; be subjected to; sustain; undergo:
归纳	guīnà	(动) sum up; conclude; induce (to form a general principle using a particular set of facts or ideas)
督促	dūcù	(动) supervise sb. and urge him to go ahead
监督	jiāndū	(动) supervise; superintend; control
供给	gōngjǐ	(动) supply; provide; furnish
支援	zhīyuán	(动) support ; give support to. (名) support; aid
赞助	zànzhù	(动) support; give assistance to; aid; sponsor
拥护	yǒnghù	(动) support; uphold ; endorse:
假设	jiǎshè	(动) suppose; assume; grant; presume (名) hypothesis

镇压	zhènyā	(动) suppress; repress; put down
压制	yāzhì	(动) suppress; stifle; inhibit:
超越	chāoyuè	(动) surmount; transcend ;surpass:
投降	tóuxiáng	(动) surrender; capitulate
探测	tàncè	(动) survey (the measuring and recording of the

details of an area of land); sound (to measure the depth of a mass of water, such as the sea, usually by sonar); probe (to examine something with a tool, especially in order to find something that is hidden); detect (to discover something, usually using special equipment)

测量	cèliáng	(动) survey; measure
中断	zhōngduàn	(动) suspend; break off; discontinue
悬念	xuánniàn	(动) suspense; be concerned about, be worried

about (sb. who is elsewhere);

(名) audience or reader involvement

吞咽	tūnyàn	(动) swallow; gulp down
摇摆	yáobǎi	(动) sway; swing; rock; vacillate :
宣誓	xuānshì	(动) swear; take an oath:

跟踪	gēnzōng	(动) tail; follow closely:
携带	xiédài	(动) take along
捎	shāo	(动) take along sth. to or for sb.:
过问	guòwèn	(动) take an interest in; concern oneself with; bother about:
发誓	fāshì	(动) take an oath; vow; pledge
保重	bǎozhòng	(动) take care of oneself
保管	bǎoguǎn	(动) take care of:
照料	zhàoliào	(动) take care of; attend to:
告辞	gàocí	(动) take leave of one' s host; bid farewell
上任	Shàngrèn	(动) take up an official post; assume office
品尝	pǐncháng	(动) taste; sample
吩咐	fēn fù	(动) tell; bid; order; instruct
试验	shìyàn	(动) test: (名) trial; experiment; test
检验	jiǎnyàn	(动) test; examine; inspect:
思索	sīsuǒ	(动) think deeply; ponder:
思念	sīniàn	(动) think of; long for; miss sb.
渴望	kěwàng	(动) thirst for; long for; yearn for; hanker after

恐吓	kǒnghè	(动) threaten; intimidate:
投掷	tóuzhí	(动) throw: hurl:
扎	zhā	(动) tie; bind
束缚	shùfù	(动) tie; bind up; fetter:
倾斜	qīngxié	(动) tilt; incline; slope; slant
参谋	cānmóu	(动) to advise 2 adviser
致使	zhìshǐ	(动) to cause; result; result in
区分	qūfēn	(动) to distinguish; (名) distinguish; differentiate
缴纳	jiǎonà	(动) to pay; to contribute,donate,hand in
向导	xiàngdǎo	(动) to show people around a place (名) tourist guide
展现	zhǎnxiàn	(动) to show; to present; to demonstrate
验证	yànzhèng	(动) to verify, to test, to justify (名) verification, verify, Validation
容忍	róngrěn	(动) tolerate; put up with:
转让	zhuǎnràng	(动) transfer one's right in sth. :
践踏	jiàntà	(动) tread on; trample underfoot:
蹬	dēng	(动) tread; tread, stamp, step up, trample

冷淡	lěngdàn	(动) treat coldly; cold-shoulder; slight
		(形) 1 cheerless; desolate 2 cold; indifferent:
款待	kuǎndài	(动) treat cordially; entertain:
亏待	kuīdài	(动) treat unfairly; treat shabbily
哆嗦	Duōsuō	(动) tremble; shiver:
捆绑	kǔnbǎng	(动) truss up; bind; tie up
信赖	xìnlài	(动) trust; have faith in:
想方设法	xiǎngfāngshèfǎ	(动) try by every means possible
力图	lìtú	(动) try hard to; strive to
拔苗助长	bámiáozhùzhǎng	(动) try to help the saplings grow by pulling them

upward--spoil things by excessive enthusiasm

扭转	niǔzhuǎn	(动) turn round:
琢磨	zhuómó	(动) turn sth. over in one's mind; ponder
缠绕	chánrào	(动) twine; bind; wind; to wrap round
闪烁	shǎnshuò	(动) twinkle; glimmer ; glisten:
拧	níng	(动) twist ; wring (to hold something tightly with

both hands and twist it by turning your hands in opposite directions)

| 领会 | lǐnghuì | (动) understand; comprehend; grasp: |

谅解	liàngjiě	(动) understand; make allowance for:
承办	chéngbàn	(动) undertake
团结	tuánjié	(动) unite; rally (to (cause to) come together in order to provide support or make a shared effort)
截至	jiézhì	(动) Up to; ended at
应邀	yìngyāo	(动) upon invitation.
借鉴	jièjiàn	(动) use for reference; benefit by another person's experience; draw on the experience of:
违背	wéibèi	(动) violate; go against; run counter to:
呕吐	ǒutù	(动) vomit; throw up
否决	fǒujué	(动) vote against; veto:
投票	tóupiào	(动) vote; cast a vote
伺候	cìhòu	(动) wait on; serve:
叮嘱	dīngzhǔ	(动) warn repeatedly; exhort
警告	jǐnggào	(动) warn; caution; admonish (名) warning (as a disciplinary measure)
告诫	gàojiè	(动) warn; exhort (to strongly encourage or try to persuade someone to do something)
糟蹋	zāotà	(动) waste; ruin; spoil 2 trample on; ravage

飘扬	piāoyáng	(动) wave; flutter (to make a series of quick delicate movements up and down or from side to side)
削弱	xuēruò	(动) weaken; cripple
编织	biānzhī	(动) weave; knit; plait; to weave a sth. from/out of grass, bamboo or rattan etc.
权衡	quánhéng	(动) weigh; balance:
呼啸	hūxiào	(动) whistle (to make a long, high sound while moving quickly through or past something); scream:
批发	pīfā	(动) wholesale
为首	wéishǒu	(动) with sb. as the leader; headed (or led) by
作息	zuòxí	(动) work and rest:
操劳	cāoláo	(动) work hard
争气	zhēngqì	(动) work hard to win honor for; try to bring credit to
锲而不舍	qiè'érbùshě	(动) work with perseverance
恶化	èhuà	(动) worsen; deteriorate:
崇拜	chóngbài	(动) worship; adore:
兜	dōu	(动) wrapped up in a piece of cloth, etc.

(名) pocket; bag:

摧残	cuīcán	(动) wreck; destroy; devastate
搏斗	bódòu	(动) wrestle ; fight ; struggle:
写作	xiězuò	(动) write:
向往	xiàngwǎng	(动) yearn for (to wish very strongly); look forward to
给予	jǐyǔ	(动)(书) give; render:
瘸	qué	(动)(口) be lame; limp:
摇滚	yáogǔn	(动)(名) rock and roll
奖赏	jiǎngshǎng	(动)(名) award; reward
发炎	fāyán	(动)(名) inflammation (causing or related to swelling and pain in the body)
按摩	ànmó	(动)(名) massage

3 Adjective 形容词 xíngróngcí

HSK 1 Adjective 形容词 xíngróngcí (9)

好	hǎo	1 (形) good; fine ; nice:
大	dà	1 (形) big; large; great
小	Xiǎo	1 (形) small; little ; petty; minor:
多	duō	1 (形) many much; more:
少	shǎo	1 (形) few; little:
冷	lěng	1 (形) cold:
热	Rè	1 (形) hot:
高兴	gāoxìng	(形) glad; happy; pleased; cheerful

| 漂亮 | piàoliang | 1 (形) handsome; good looking; pretty: |

HSK 2 Adjective 形容词 xíngróngcí (19)

高	gāo	(形) 1 tall; high:
红	hóng	1 (形) 1 red:
白	bái	(形) 1 snow-white:
黑	hēi	1 (形) black:
忙	máng	1 (形) busy; fully occupied:
快	kuài	1 (形) 1 fast; quick; rapid:
慢	màn	1 (形) slow:
远	yuǎn	1 (形) 1 far; distant; remote:
近	jìn	1 (形) near; close:
好吃	hào chī	(形) nice; delicious

累	lèi	(形) tired; fatigued; weary:
长	cháng	1 (形) long:
新	xīn	(形) new; fresh; up-to-date:
贵	guì	1 (形) expensive; costly; dear:
便宜	piányí	1 (形) cheap; inexpensive:
晴	qíng	(形) fine; clear
阴	yīn	6 (形) cloudy; overcast
错	cuò	2 (形) 1 wrong; mistaken; erroneous:
快乐	kuàilè	(形) happy; joyful; cheerful

HSK 3 Adjective 形容词 xíngróngcí (37)

低	dī	1 (形) low:
短	duǎn	1 (形) short; brief :
饿	è	1 (形) hungry:
方便	fāngbiàn	1 (形) 1 convenient:
干净	gānjìng	(形) 1 clean:
坏	huài	1 (形) bad:
简单	jiǎndān	(形) 1 simple; uncomplicated:
久	jiǔ	(形) 1 for a long time; long
旧	jiù	1 (形) past; old fashioned; old:
渴	kě	1 (形) thirsty:
可爱	Kě'ài	(形) lovable; lovely:
老	lǎo	1 (形) old; aged:
矮	ǎi	(形) 1 short (of stature)
难	nán	1 (形) hard; difficult:
年轻	niánqīng	(形) young:
胖	pàng	(形) fat; stout; plump: chubby

奇怪	qíguài	(形) strange; odd; surprising:
认真	rènzhēn	1 (形) conscientious; earnest; serious:
容易	róngyì	1 (形) easy:
瘦	shòu	1 (形) thin
舒服	shūfú	1 (形) comfortable
疼	téng	1 (动) ache; pain; sore:
甜	tián	1 (形) sweet; honeyed

相同	xiāngtóng	(形) identical; the same
小心!	xiǎoxīn!	(形) Be carefull or Watch out!
新鲜	xīnxiān	(形) fresh:
一样	yīyàng	(形) the same; equally; alike:
一般	yībān	(形) 2 general; ordinary; common:
有名	yǒumíng	(形) well known; famous; renowned; celebrated

差	chà	(形) 4 not up to standard; poor.

质量不算太差　　　zhìliàng bù suàn tài chà　The quality is not too bad

差	chà	1 (动) differ from; fall short of
重要	zhòngyào	(形) important; significant; major:
主要	zhǔyào	(形) main; major; chief; principal:
总是	zǒng shì	(形) always
安静	ānjìng	(形) quiet; peaceful:
聪明	cōngmíng	(形) intelligent; bright; clever:
当然	dāngrán	(形) of course; without doubt:

HSK 4 Adjective 形容词 xíngróngcí (100)

暗	àn	(形)[12] dark; dim; dull:
笨	bèn	(形) low; stupid; thick:
差不多	chàbùduō	(形) almost; nearly:
诚实	chéngshí	(形) honest
成熟	chéngshú	(形) ripe; mature:

[12] (形) indicates 形容词　xíngróngcí　　Adjective

粗心	cūxīn	(形) careless; thoughtless:
得意	déyì	(形) complacent:
对	duì	(形) correct; right:
富	fù	(形) rich; wealthy; abundant
复杂	fùzá	(形) complicated; complex
干燥	gānzào	(形) dry; arid:
高级	gāojí	(形) senior; high-ranking; high-level:
共同	gòngtóng	(形) common:
够	gòu	(形) enough; sufficient; adequate:
孤单	gūdān	(形) alone:
国际	guójì	(形) international:
害羞	hàixiū	(形) feel ashamed
合格	hégé	(形) up to standard
合适	Héshì	(形) suitable; appropriate; becoming; right:
厚	hòu	(形) thick:
活泼	huópō	(形) lively; vivacious; vivid:
假	jiǎ	(形) false; fake; artificial

骄傲	jiāo'ào	(形) arrogant; conceited:
激动	jīdòng	(形) excitedemotional (动) excite; stir:
积极	jījí	(形) positive 2 active; energetic; vigorous
精彩	jīngcǎi	(形) brilliant; splendid; wonderful:
紧张	jǐnzhāng	(形) nervous; in a flurry:
及时	jíshí	(形) timely; in good time:
可怜	kělián	(形) pitiful; pitiable; poor:
可惜	kěxí	(形) it's a pity; it's too bad:
苦	kǔ	(形) bitter 2 (名) hardship; suffering; pain
宽	kuān	(形) 1 wide; broad:
困	kùn	(形) tired(形) 2 (动) be stranded: be hard pressed:
辣	là	(形) peppery; hot; spicy
懒	lǎn	(形) lazy; indolent; slothful
浪漫	làngmàn	(形) romantic
冷静	lěngjìng	(形) sober; calm :
亮	liàng	(形) light; bright; shiny
凉快	liángkuai	(形) nice and cool
厉害	lìhài	(形) powerful; (名) serious damage (名) power.

流利	liúlì	(形) fluent; smooth:
流行	liúxíng	(形) prevalent; popular; fashionable; in vogue
乱	luàn	(形) in disorder ; in a confusion:
马虎	mǎhǔ	(形) careless; casual:
满	mǎn	(形) full; filled ; packed:
美丽	měilì	(形) beautiful
免费	miǎnfèi	(形) free of charge ; free:
难受	nánshòu	(形) feel unwell; feel uncomfortable:
暖和	nuǎnhuo	(形) warm; nice and warm
普通	pǔtōng	(形) ordinary; common; average:
轻	qīng	(形) light (in weight) :
轻松	qīngsōng	(形) relaxed:
穷	qióng	(形) poor; poverty-stricken
全部	quánbù	(形) (名) all; whole; complete; total:
热闹	rènào	(形) lively; bustling with noise and excitement:
软	ruǎn	(形) soft; flexible:
伤心	shāngxīn	(形) sad; grieved; brokenhearted:

深	shēn	(形) deep:
适合	shìhé	(形) proper (动) suit ; fit:
实际	shíjì	(形) 1 practical; realistic: 1 real; actual; concrete 3(名) reality; practice :
湿润	shīrùn	(形) moist
实在	shízài	(形) true; real; honest; dependable:
帅	shuài	(形) beautiful; graceful; smart; handsome
顺利	shùnlì	(形) smoothly; successfully:
随便	suíbiàn	(形) casual; random; informal:
危险	wéixiǎn	(形) dangerous; perilous: (名) danger;
无聊	wúliáo	(形) falling in a vacant mood; bored
咸	xián	(形) salty; salted:
响	xiǎng	(形) 1 loud; noisy 2 (动) sound; make a sound 3 (名) sound; noise
香	xiāng	(形) (of flower etc.) fragrant; scented 2(of food) delicious; appetizing
相反	xiāngfǎn	(形) opposite; contrary:
详细	xiángxì	(形) detailed; minute:
兴奋	xīngfèn	(形) be excited

辛苦	xīnkǔ	(形) hard; hardworking:
许多	xǔduō	(形) many; much; a lot of
严格	yángé	(形) strict; rigorous; rigid:
严重	yánzhòng	(形) serious; grave; critical:
硬	yìng	(形) hard; stiff; tough:
幽默	yōumò	(形) humorous:
有趣	yǒuqù	(形) interesting; delightful; amusing
圆	yuán	(形) round; circular; spherical:
原来	yuánlái	(形) original ; former:
愉快	yúkuài	(形) happy; joyful; cheerful
脏	zàng	(形) dirty; filthy
窄	zhǎi	(形) narrow:
暂时	zhànshí	(形) temporary; transient:
正常	zhèngcháng	(形) normal; regular:
正好	zhènghǎo	(形) just in time ; just right; just enough:
整齐	zhěngqí	(形) neat and tidy
正确	zhèngquè	(形) correct
正式	zhèngshì	(形) formal; official; regular:

真正	zhēnzhèng	(形) genuine; true; real:
直接	zhí jiē	(形) direct; immediate:
专门	zhuānmén	(形) special; specialized:
著名	zhù míng	(形) famous; well-known:
准确	zhǔnquè	(形) precise ; accurate ; exact:
准时	zhǔnshí	(形) punctual; on time:
仔细	zǐxì	(形) careful; attentive:
最好	zuì hǎo	(形) best; first-rate: 2 (副) had better; it would be best:
勇敢	yǒnggǎn	(形) brave; courageous:
优秀	yōuxiù	(形) outstanding; excellent; splendid:

HSK 5 Adjective 形容词 xíngróngcí (182)

乖	guāi	(形) (of a child) well-behaved; obedient:
正	zhèng	(形) straight; upright:
苗条	miáotiáo	(形) (of a woman) slender; slim

激烈 acute:	jīliè	(形) (of action and argument) intense; sharp; fierce;
巧妙	qiǎomiào	(形) (of methods, skills, etc.) ingenious; clever
基本	jīběn	(形) 1 basic; fundamental:
便	biàn	(形) 1 convenient; handy: 3 informal;plain; ordinary
淡	dàn	(形) 1 thin; light (形) 2 tasteless; weak; bland
片面	piànmiàn	(形) 1 unilateral 2 one-sided:
所谓	suǒwèi	(形) 1 what is called:
能干	nénggàn	(形) able; capable; competent
绝对	juéduì	(形) absolute:
抽象	chōuxiàng	(形) abstract:
偶然	ǒurán	(形) accidental; fortuitous; chance:
了不起	liǎobùqǐ	(形) amazing ; terrific:
古老	gǔlǎo	(形) ancient; age-old
艰苦	jiānkǔ	(形) arduous; difficult; hard; tough:
艰巨	jiānjù	(形) arduous; extremely difficult:
照常	zhàocháng	(形) as usual
歪	wāi	(形) askew; crooked; inclined; slanting:

刻苦	kèkǔ	(形) assiduous; hardworking; painstaking
临时	línshí	(形) at the time when sth. happens:
自动	zìdòng	(形) automatic
平均	píngjūn	(形) average:
恶劣	èliè	(形) bad; evil; disgusting:
根本	gēnběn	(形) basic ; fundamental; essential :
专心	zhuānxīn	(形) be attentive; be absorbed:
好奇	hàoqí	(形) be curious:
自豪	zìháo	(形) be proud of; take pride in:
有利	Yǒulì	(形) beneficial; advantageous:
瞎	xiā	(形) blind
模糊	móhú	(形) blurred; indistinct; dim; vague:
鲜艳	xiānyàn	(形) bright- coloured:
光明	guāngmíng	(形) bright; promising:
活跃	huóyuè	(形) brisk: active; dynamic:
平静	píngjìng	(形) calm; quiet; tranquil:
无奈	wúnài	(形) cannot help but; have no alternative:
古典	gǔdiǎn	(形) classical

明确	míngquè	(形) clear and definite; unequivocal:
明显	míngxiǎn	(形) clear; obvious :
密切	mìqiè	(形) close; intimate:
舒适	shūshì	(形) comfortable
完整	Wánzhěng	(形) complete; integrated; intact:
具体	jùtǐ	(形) concrete; specific; particular (as opposed to abstract) :
亲切	qīnqiè	(形) cordial; warm
日常	rìcháng	(形) day-to-day; everyday:
亲爱	qīn'ài	(形) dear; beloved
不得了	bùdéliao	(形) desperately serious; disastrous:
发达	fādá	(形) developed; flourishing:
勤奋	qínfèn	(形) diligent; hard-working
勤劳	qínláo	(形) diligent; industrious:
醉	zuì	(形) drunk; inebriated
初级	chūjí	(形) elementary; primary:
均匀	jūnyún	(形) even; well distributed:

过分	guòfèn	(形) excessive; going too far; overdone
疲劳	píláo	(形) exhausted; weary
广泛	guǎngfàn	(形) extensive; wide-ranging; widespread:
多余	duōyú	(形) extra; surplus:
公平	gōngpíng	(形) fair; just; impartial; equitable :
时髦	shímáo	(形) fashionable; stylish; in vogue:
可怕	kěpà	(形) fearful; frightful; terrible; terrifying:
惭愧	cánkuì	(形) feel ashamed:
坚决	jiānjué	(形) firm; resolute; determined:
平	píng	(形) flat; level; even; smooth:
繁荣	fánróng	(形) flourishing; prosperous; booming:
慌张	huāngzhāng	(形) flurried; flustered; confused:
幸运	xìngyùn	(形) fortunate; lucky:
坦率	tǎnshuài	(形) frank
干脆	gāncuì	(形) frank and straight forward:
充分	chōngfèn	(形) full; ample; abundant:
通常	tōngcháng	(形) general; usual; normal:
温柔	wēnróu	(形) gentle and soft

善良	shànliáng	(形) good and honest; kindhearted
良好	liánghǎo	(形) good:
优美	yōuměi	(形) graceful; fine; exquisite:
伟大	wěidà	(形) great; mighty
灰	huī	(形) grey (名) ash; dust
匆忙	cōngmáng	(形) hastily; in a hurry:
重	zhòng	(形) heavy
英俊	yīngjùn	(形) highly talented; brilliant
老实	lǎoshí	(形) honest; frank:
荣幸	róngxìng	(形) honoured:
横	héng	(形) horizontal; transverse:
巨大	jùdà	(形) huge; tremendous; enormous; gigantic; immense:
一致	yīzhì	(形) identical; consistent:
不耐烦	bù nàifán	(形) impatient
急忙	jímáng	(形) in a hurry; in haste; hurriedly; hastily:
糟糕	zāogāo	(形) in a terrible mess; bad luck; too bad:
个别	gèbié	(形) individual:
必然	bìrán	(形) inevitable; certain:

天真	tiānzhēn	(形) innocent; simple and unaffected; naive:
无数	wúshù	(形) innumerable; countless:
不要紧	bùyàojǐn	(形) it doesn't matter; never mind; it's not serious
大型	dàxíng	(形) large; large-scale:
合法	héfǎ	(形) legal; lawful; legitimate; rightful:
次要	cì yào	(形) less important; secondary; minor
青	qīng	(形) light blue or dark green: 2 young (people)
清淡	qīngdàn	(形) light; delicate:
生动	shēngdòng	(形) lively; vivid:
寂寞	jìmò	(形) lonely; lonesome:
悠久	yōujiǔ	(形) long; long-standing; age-old
豪华	háohuá	(形) luxurious; sumptuous:
雄伟	xióngwěi	(形) magnificent; majestic
小气	xiǎoqì	(形) mean; stingy
谦虚	qiānxū	(形) modest; self-effacing:
单调	dāndiào	(形) monotonous; dull; drab:
糊涂	hútú	(形) muddle-headed; confused; bewildered:
神秘	shénmì	(形) mysterious

大方	dàfāng	(形) natural and poised; unaffected:
调皮	tiáopí	(形) naughty; mischievous
灵活	línghuó	(形) nimble; agile; quick:
不足	bùzú	(形) not enough; insufficient; inadequate:
客观	kèguān	(形) objective:
显然	xiǎnrán	(形) obvious; evident
高档	gāodàng	(形) of top grade quality:
纷纷	fēnfēn	(形) one after another; in succession:
唯一	wéi yī	(形) only; sole: (samse as 惟一).
公开	gōngkāi	(形) open; overt; public:
虚心	xūxīn	(形) open-minded; modest; modest and

unassuming

乐观	lèguān	(形) optimistic; hopeful; sanguine:
突出	túchū	(形) outstanding; prominent:
出色	chūsè	(形) outstanding; remarkable; splendid
完善	wánshàn	(形) perfect; complete:
完美	wánměi	(形) perfect; consummate:
悲观	bēiguān	(形) pessimistic:

实用	shíyòng	(形) practical; pragmatic:
优惠	yōuhuì	(形) preferential; favorable:
私人	sīrén	(形) private; personal:
谨慎	jǐnshèn	(形) prudent; careful; cautlous; circumspect:
紫	zǐ	(形) purple
合理	hélǐ	(形) rational; reasonable; equitable:
可靠	kěkào	(形) reliable; trustworthy
必要	bìyào	(形) requisite; necessary; indispensable:
沉默	chénmò	(形) reticent; uncommunicative:
秘密	mìmì	(形) secret; confidential (名) secret
自私	zìsī	(形) selfish; self-centred; egoistic
浅	qiǎn	(形) shallow:
尖锐	jiānruì	(形) sharp-pointed
相似	xiāngsì	(形) similar
朴素	pǔsù	(形) simple; plain:
单纯	dānchún	(形) simple; pure:
诚恳	chéngkěn	(形) sincere:
熟练	shúliàn	(形) skilled; practised; proficient:

斜	xié	(形) slanting; inclined:
呆	dāi	(形) slow-witted; dull:
狡猾	jiǎohuá	(形) sly; crafty; cunning; tricky
臭	chòu	(形) smelly; stinking; foul:
光滑	guānghuá	(形) smooth; glossy; sleek
严肃	yánsù	(形) solemn; serious; grave
结实	jiēshi	(形) solid; sturdy; durable:
迅速	xùnsù	(形) speedy; rapid:
方	fāng	(形) square:
稳定	wěndìng	(形) stable; steady:
直	zhí	(形) straight
陌生	mòshēng	(形) strange; unfamiliar: -
坚强	jiānqiáng	(形) strong; firm; staunch:
强烈	qiángliè	(形) strong; intense; violent:
傻	shǎ	(形) stupid; muddle- headed:
主观	zhǔguān	(形) subjective:
嫩	nèn	(形) tender; delicate:
浓	nóng	(形) thick; dense; concentrated:

薄	báo	(形) thin; flimsy
彻底	chèdǐ	(形) thorough; thoroughgoing
周到	zhōudào	(形) thoughtful; considerate:
透明	tòumíng	(形) transparent:
真实	zhēnshí	(形) true; real; actual; authentic:
不安	bù'ān	(形) turbulent; unstable:
丑	chǒu	(形) ugly
难看	nánkàn	(形) ugly
独特	dútè	(形) unique; distinctive:
迫切	pòqiè	(形) urgen t; pressing:
紧急	jǐnjí	(形) urgent; pressing; critical
宝贵	bǎoguì	(形) valuable; precious:
广大	guǎngdà	(形) vast; wide; extensive
温暖	wēnnuǎn	(形) warm;
热心	rèxīn	(形) warm-hearted; enthuslastlc:
弱	ruò	(形) weak; feeble :
整个	zhěnggè	(形) whole; entire:
疯狂	fēngkuáng	(形) wild , crazy, frenzied:

特殊	tèshū	（形）special; particular; peculiar; exceptional :
痛快	tòngkuài	（形）very happy; delighted; overjoyed:
热烈	rèliè	（形）warm; enthusiastic; ardent:

HSK 6 Adjective 形容词 xíngróngcí (428)

常务	chángwù	（形）day-to-day business; routine:
鲜明	xiānmíng	（形）(of colour) bright:
特定	tèdìng	（形）specially designated (or appointed) 2 specific; specified; given
漫长	màncháng	（形）very long; endless:
兢兢业业	jīngjīng yè yè	（形）(act) with caution and with a will
贤惠	xiánhuì	（形）(of a woman) capable; virtuous
无微不至	wúwēibùzhì	（形）(of cares, concern) meticulous; in every possible way:
锋利	fēnglì	（形）(of knives, etc.) sharp; keen
平坦	Píngtǎn	（形）(of land, etc.) level; even; smooth:
耀眼	yàoyǎn	（形）(of light) dazzling
齐全	qíquán	（形）(of stock, etc.) complete:

干旱	gānhàn	(形) (of weather or soil) arid; dry
沉闷	chénmèn	(形) 1 (of weather, atmosphere, etc.) oppressive 2 depressed; in low spirits:
千方百计	qiānfāngbǎijì	(形) (副) in a hundred and one ways; by every conceivable means.
喜悦	xǐyuè	(形) (名) happy; joyous (full of joy)
正经	zhèngjīng	(形) 1 decent; respectable; honest: 2 serious
霸道	bàdào	(形) 1 (feudal) rule by force 2 savage; high-handed:
慢性	mànxìng	(形) 1 chronic 2 slow (in taking effect)
深沉	shēnchén	(形) 1 dark; deep: 2 (of sound or voice) deep; dull 3 concealing one's real feelings
腐烂	fǔlàn	(形) 1 decomposed 2 corrupt; rotten:
浓厚	nónghòu	(形) 1 dense; thick 2 (of atmosphere; colour. interest. etc.) strong
急切	jíqiè	(形) 1 eager; impatient 2 in a hurry; in haste
盛	shèng	(形) 1 flourishing; prosperous 2 vigorous; energetic 3 magnificent; grand 4 abundant; plentiful 5 popular; common; widespread
慷慨	kāngkǎi	(形) 1 generous; liberal (giving or given in a generous way) 2 vehement; fervent

难得	Nándé	(形) 1 hard to come by; rare; 2 seldom; rarely:
急躁	jízào	(形) 1 irritable; irascible (made angry easily) 2 impetuous; rash; impatient:
狭窄	xiázhǎi	(形) 1 narrow; cramped 2 narrow and limited
消极	xiāojí	(形) 1 negative 2 passive; inactive
生疏	shēngshū	(形) 1 not familiar 2 out of practice; rusty
原始	yuánshǐ	(形) 1 original; firsthand : 2 primeval; primitive
纯粹	Chúncuì	(形) 1 pure; unadulterated 2 simply; purely
爽快	shuǎngkuài	(形) 1 relaxed; refreshed 2 frank; straightforward; outright
腐败	fǔbài	(形) 1 rotten; decayed
朴实	pǔshí	(形) 1 simple; plain 2 sincere and honest
僵硬	jiāngyìng	(形) 1 stiff 2 rigid; inflexible
闭塞	bìsè	(形) 1 stop up; block: 2 hard to get to; out-of-the-way; inaccessible: 3 ill informed
温和	wēnhé	(形) 1 temperate; mild; moderate 2 gentle; mild
不像话	bù xiànghuà	(形) 1 unreasonable: 2 shocking; outrageous
亲热	qīnrè	(形) 1 warm and affectionate; 2 on intimate terms
十足	shízú	(形) 100 per cent; out-and-out; sheer; downright:

曲折	qūzhé	(形) 2 winding 2 not straight or smooth; tortuous (名) complications
茫茫	mángmáng	(形) a boundless expanse of; vast:
得天独厚	détiāndúhòu	(形) abound in gifts of nature
深奥	shēn'ào	(形) abstruse; profound
荒唐	huāngtáng	(形) absurd; fantastic; preposterous:
荒谬	huāngmiù	(形) absurd; preposterous:
难能可贵	nánnéngkěguì	(形) accomplish something difficult and so deserve praise; estimable; commendable
精确	jīngquè	(形) accurate; exact; precise:
不得已	bùdéyǐ	(形) act against one's will; have no alternative but to; cannot help but:
肆无忌惮	sìwújìdàn	(形) act wildly in defiance of law and public opinion; be unscrupulous
小心翼翼	xiǎoxīnyìyì	(形) act with exceptional caution; act very cautiously
充足	chōngzú	(形) adequate; ample; sufficient; abundant:
先进	xiānjìn	(形) advanced
可行	Kěxíng	(形) advisable; feasible (able to be made, done, or achieved)

附属	fùshǔ	(形) affiliated; attached:
衰老	shuāilǎo	(形) aged; senile
含糊	hánhú	(形) ambiguous (having or expressing more than one possible meaning, sometimes intentionally); vague (not clearly expressed, known, described, or decided)
暧昧	àimèi	(形) ambiguous; equivocal:
恼火	nǎohuǒ	(形) annoyed; irritated; vexed
焦急	jiāojí	(形) anxious and restless; worried
妥当	tuǒdang	(形) appropriate; proper:
妥善	tuǒshàn	(形) appropriate; proper; well arranged:
众所周知	zhòngsuǒzhōuzhī	(形) as is known to all; as everyone knows
尴尬	gāngà	(形) awkward; embarrassed:
卑鄙	bēibǐ	(形) base (not showing any honour and having no morals); amoral; despicable:
丢三落四	diūsānlàsì	(形) be always forgetting things
反感	Fǎngǎn	(形) be averse to; repugnant (very unpleasant, causing a feeling of disgust); disgusted with (sb. or sth.)
一目了然	yīmùliǎorán	(形) be clear at a glance
无理取闹	wúlǐqǔnào	(形) be deliberately provocative

狼狈	lángbèi	(形) be embarrassed
兴高采烈	xìnggāocǎiliè	(形) be filled with joy; jubilant
欣慰	xīnwèi	(形) be gratified
好客	hàokè	(形) be hospitable
融洽	róngqià	(形) be in good terms
举世闻名	jǔshì wénmíng	(形) be known all over the world; enjoy a worldwide reputation
一丝不苟	yīsībùgǒu	(形) be very scrupulous; be very meticulous
美观	měiguān	(形) beautiful; artistic; pleasing to the eye:
荒凉	huāngliáng	(形) bleak and desolate; wild:
盲目	mángmù	(形) blind; unchecked; unwarranted (副) blindly; unrealistically; indiscriminately
豪迈	háomài	(形) bold; heroic :
天生	tiānshēng	(形) born; inborn; inherent; innate:
崭新	zhǎnxīn	(形) brand new; completely new
壮烈	zhuàngliè	(形) brave; heroic:
灿烂	cànlàn	(形) bright; magnificent; splendid; brilliant

卓越	zhuóyuè	(形) brilliant; outstanding:
辉煌	huīhuáng	(形) brilliant; splendid; glorious:
刻不容缓	kèbùrónghuǎn	(形) brook no delay; demand immediate attention; be very urgent
繁忙	fánmáng	(形) busy:
忙碌	mánglù	(形) busy; bustling about
镇定	zhèndìng	(形) calm and composed
安详	ānxiáng	(形) calm; composcd; placid (having a calm appearance or characteristics)
镇静	zhènjìng	(形) calm; cool; composed; unruffled:
得力	délì	(形) capable; competent:
无忧无虑	wú yōu wú lǜ	(形) carefree
细致	Xìzhì	(形) careful; meticulous:
周密	zhōumì	(形) carefully considered; meticulous (very careful and with great attention to every detail)
草率	cǎoshuài	(形) careless; rash:
慎重	shènzhòng	(形) cautious; careful; prudent; discreet
博大精深	bódàjīngshēn	(形) characterized by extensive knowledge and profound scholarship

迷人	mírén	(形) Charming; enchanting; fascinating
幼稚	yòuzhì	(形) childish; naive
清洁	qīngjié	(形) clean
澄清	chéngqīng	(形) clear; transparent

清醒   qīngxǐng   (形) clear-headed; sane (showing good judgment and understanding); sharp mind

(动) regain consciousness

分明   Fēnmíng   (形) clearly distinguished; distinct (副) clearly; plainly; evidently

伶俐	línglì	(形) clever; bright; quick witted
机灵	jīling	(形) clever; smart; quickminded
临床	línchuáng	(形) clinical:
紧密	jǐnmì	(形) close together; inseparable:
笨拙	bènzhuō	(形) clumsy; awkward; stupid:
完备	wánbèi	(形) complete; all ready
简要	jiǎnyào	(形) concise and to the point; brief:

可观	Kěguān	(形) considerable; impressive; sizable:
一贯	yīguàn	(形) consistent; persistent; all along:
便利	biànlì	(形) convenient; easy:
沉着	chénzhuó	(形) cool-headed; composed; calm; steady:
对应	duìyìng	(形) corresponding
相应	xiāngyìng	(形) corresponding; relevant
残酷	cánkù	(形) cruel; brutal; ruthless
残忍	cánrěn	(形) cruel; ruthless
清澈	qīngchè	(形) crystal clear
聋哑	lóng yǎ	(形) deaf and dumb; deafmute.
根深蒂固	gēnshēndìgù	(形) deep-rooted; inveterate
确切	quèqiè	(形) definite; exact; precise
沮丧	jǔsàng	(形) dejected; depressed; dispirited; discouraged:
稠密	chóumì	(形) dense:
辩证	biànzhèng	(形) dialectical (discovering what is true by

considering opposite theories)

艰难	jiānnán	(形) difficult; hard:
勤恳	qínkěn	(形) diligent and conscientious:

遥远	yáoyuǎn	(形) distant; remote:
清晰	qīngxī	(形) distinct; clear:
凄凉	qīliáng	(形) dreary; miserable
枯竭	kūjié	(形) dried up; exhausted:
枯燥	kūzào	(形) dull and dry ; uninteresting:
耐用	nàiyòng	(形) durable:
急功近利	jígōngjìnlì	(形) eager for instant success and quick profit
恳切	kěnqiè	(形) earnest; sincere:
轻而易举	qīng'éryìjǔ	(形) easy to accomplish
文雅	wényǎ	(形) Elegant; refined; cultured
难堪	nánkān	(形) embarrassed:
层出不穷	céngchūbùqióng	(形) emerge in an endless stream; come thick and fast
空洞	kōngdòng	(形) empty; hollow (名) cavity
无穷无尽	wúqióng wújìn	(形) endless; inexhaustible
开明	kāimíng	(形) enlightened; liberal; open-minded
不相上下	bù xiāng shàngxià	(形) equally matched; roughly the same :
永恒	yǒnghéng	(形) eternal; everlasting

优异	yōuyì	(形) excellent; outstanding; exceedingly good:
额外	éwài	(形) extra; additional:
极端	jíduān	(形) extreme; exceeding:
忠实	zhōngshí	(形) faithful; reliable:
虚假	xūjiǎ	(形) false; sham
忧郁	yōuyù	(形) feel depressed or frustrated
凶恶	xiōng'è	(形) ferocious and vicious; fiendish
肥沃	féiwò	(形) fertile; rich
封建	fēngjiàn	(形) feudal (relating to the social system of that is

organized according to rank.)

精致	jīngzhì	(形) fine; exquisite; delicate
晴朗	qínglǎng	(形) fine; sunny
坚韧	jiānrèn	(形) firm and tenacious
牢固	láogù	(形) firm; secure:
坚固	jiāngù	(形) firm; solid; sturdy; strong:
坚定	jiāndìng	(形) firm; staunch; steadfast:
一流	yīliú	(形) First-class; Superb
合身	héshēn	(形) fit (to be the right size or shape for someone

or something)

扁	biǎn	(形) flat
机动	jīdòng	(形) flexible; expedient; mobile 2 in reserve; for emergency use:
繁华	fánhuá	(形) flourishing; bustling; busy:
欣欣向荣	xīnxīnxiàngróng	(形) flourishing; thriving
川流不息	chuānliúbùxī	(形) flow past in an end less stream; come in a never-ending stream
聚精会神	jùjīnghuìshén	(形) focus one's attention; be all intent
民用	mínyòng	(形) forcivil use; civil:
原先	yuánxiān	(形) former; original:
零星	língxīng	(形) fragmentary; odd; piecemeal:
坦白	tǎnbái	(形) frank and straightforward
无偿	wúcháng	(形) free; gratis; gratuitous:
频繁	pínfán	(形) frequently; often:
丰满	fēngmǎn	(形) full and round; well-developed; full- grown:
朝气蓬勃	zhāoqì péngbó	(形) full of vigour
和气	héqì	(形) gentle; kind; polite; good-natured (名) harmonious relationship
半途而废	bàntú'érfèi	(形) (成语[13])give up halfway

物美价廉	wùměi jià lián	(形) good and inexpensive
拿手	náshǒu	(形) good at; adept; expert:
可口	kěkǒu	(形) good to eat; nice; tasty; palatable
隆重	lóngzhòng	(形) grand; solemn; ceremomous:
油腻	yóunì	(形) grease; oily; heavy
谗	chán	(形) greedy; gluttonous
悲哀	bēi'āi	(形) grieved ; sorrowful
主导	zhǔdǎo	(形) guiding; leading; dominant:
秃	tū	(形) hairless; bald 2 bare
欢乐	huānlè	(形) happy and gay; merry:
舒畅	shūchàng	(形) happy; entirely free from worry :
快活	kuàihuó	(形) happy; merry; cheerful
美满	měimǎn	(形) happy; perfectly satisfactory:
难免	nánmiǎn	(形) hard to avoid; unavoidable

[13]成语 chéngyǔ (名) idiom; proverb; set phrase. The whole set of Chinese Culture Stories Series, idiom; proverb; set phrases, 41 books @ $ 2.4/BOOK ONLY!, 1050 articles, 18 categories. Chinese-English bilingual, Detailed explanations and expansions of Vocabularies, Perfect for HSK 4-6, IGCSE Chinese, IB Chinese & School extra readings. Find the QR code on the first page for the best price for the whole set of books. New launching BEST price at http://edeo.biz/26749

坚硬	jiān yìng	(形) hard; solid
勤俭	qínjiǎn	(形) hard-working and thrifty:
用功	yònggōng	(形) hardworking; diligent; studious:
和谐	héxié	(形) harmonious (friendly and peaceful)

和睦　hémù　(形) harmonious; amicable (relating to behaviour between people that is pleasant and friendly, often despite a difficult situation 心平气和的；不伤和气的)

可恶　kěwù　(形) hateful; abominable (very bad or unpleasant); detestable (people or things that you hate very much)

| 自卑 | zìbēi | (形) have inferiority complex: |
| 优先 | yōuxiān | (形) have priority; take precedence: |

见多识广　jiàn duō shì guǎng　(形) have wide experience and extensive knowledge

腥	xīng	(形) having fishy smell
衷心	zhōngxīn	(形) Heartfelt; cordial; wholehearted
沉重	chénzhòng	(形) heavy:
举足轻重	jǔzúqīngzhòng	(形) hold the balance; play a decisive role:
空虚	kōngxū	(形) hollow; void

廉洁	liánjié	(形) honest (honest or fair, or showing that you have not done anything illegal); with clean hands; whitehanded; not corrupt
庞大	pángdà	(形) huge; enormous; colossal:
人为	rénwéi	(形) human made (名) human effort:
饥	jī	(形) hungry; starvying;
仓促	cāngcù	(形) hurriedly; hastily:
虚伪	xūwèi	(形) hypocritical; false
称心如意	chènxīn rúyì	(形) ideal; after one's own heart.
愚昧	yúmèi	(形) ignorant (not having enough knowledge, understanding, or information about something)
无知	wúzhī	(形) ignorant:
茫然	mángrán	(形) ignorant; in the dark; at a loss:
非法	fēifǎ	(形) illegal; unlawful:
威风	wēifēng	(形) 1 imposing; impressive; awe inspiring (名) 2 power and prestige
慌忙	huāngmáng	(形) in a great rush; in a flurry; hurriedly
络绎不绝	luòyì bù jué	(形) in an endless stream:

通用	tōngyòng	(形) in common use; current; general 2 interchangeable:
兴致勃勃	xìngzhì bóbó	(形) in high spirits.
有条不紊	yǒutiáobùwěn	(形) in perfect order; orderly
无比	wúbǐ	(形) incomparable; unparalleled; matchless:
莫名其妙	mòmíngqímiào	(形) incomprehensible.
不可思议	bùkěsīyì	(形) inconceivable; Unimaginable
间接	jiànjiē	(形) indirect; second-hand:
隐约	yǐnyuē	(形) indistinct; faint:
辛勤	xīnqín	(形) industrious; hard-working
初步	chūbù	(形) initial; preliminary; tentative:
刹那	chànà	(形) instant
智能	zhìnéng	(形) Intelligent
固有	gùyǒu	(形) intrinsic; inherent; innate:
内在	nèizài	(形) intrinsic; inherent; internal:
清真	qīngzhēn	(形) Islamic; Muslim: Halal
孤立	gūlì	(形) isolated:
无可奈何	wúkěnàihé	(形) it can't be helped

不言而喻	bù yán ér yù	(形) it goes without saying; it is self-evident
公正	gōngzhèng	(形) just; fair; impartial
一举两得	yījǔliǎngdé	(形) kill two birds with one stone
慈祥	cíxiáng	(形) kind; amiable; benevolent
和蔼	Hé'ǎi	(形) kindly; amiable; affable
伤脑筋	shāng nǎojīn	(形) knotty; troublesome; bothersome
持久	chíjiǔ	(形) lasting; enduring :
可笑	kěxiào	(形) laughable; ridiculous (stupid or unreasonable and deserving to be laughed at); ludicrous; funny:
懒惰	lǎnduò	(形) lazy
无精打采	wújīngdǎcǎi	(形) listless; crestfallen; in low spirits
崇高	chónggāo	(形) lofty; high:
孤独	gūdú	(形) lonely; solitary :
啰嗦	luōsuo	(形) long-winded; wordy:
丢人	diūrén	(形) lose face; Disgraced; Shame
响亮	xiǎngliàng	(形) loud and clear; resounding; resonant
喜闻乐见	xǐwénlèjiàn	(形) love to see and hear; be enjoyed by
忠诚	zhōngchéng	(形) loyal; faithful

吉祥	jíxiáng	(形) lucky; auspicious (suggesting a positive and successful future); propitious (likely to result in success, or showing signs of success)
茂盛	màoshèng	(形) luxuriant; thriving; flourishing
奢侈	shēchǐ	(形) luxurious (very comfortable and expensive); extravagant (spending too much money)
宏观	hóngguān	(形) macro (large; relating to the whole of something, rather than its parts)
神奇	shénqí	(形) magical; mystical; miraculous
壮丽	zhuànglì	(形) magnificent and enchanting; majestic:
华丽	huálì	(形) magnificent; resplendent; gorgeous:
人工	réngōng	(形) man-made; artificial:
显著	xiǎnzhe	(形) marked; remarkable:
奇妙	qímiào	(形) marvelous; wonderful; intriguing (very interesting because of being unusual or mysterious)
微观	wéiguān	(形) microcosmic:
起码	qǐmǎ	(形) minimum; rudimentary; elementary:
悲惨	bēicǎn	(形) miserable; tragic:
谦逊	qiānxùn	(形) modest and unassuming
潮湿	cháoshī	(形) moist; damp

尖端	jiānduān	(形) most advanced; sophisticated
浑浊	húnzhuó	(形) muddy; turbid [(of a liquid) not transparent]
狭隘	xiá'ài	(形) narrow
淘气	táoqì	(形) naughty; mischievous:
高尚	gāoshàng	(形) noble; lofty
嘈杂	cáozá	(形) noisy:
新颖	xīnyǐng	(形) novel and original:
别致	biézhì	(形) novel; delightful:
麻木	mámù	(形) numb:
顽固	wángù	(形) obstinate; stubborn; headstrong:
古怪	gǔguài	(形) odd; eccentric (strange or unusual, sometimes in a humorous way)
平行	píngxíng	(形) of equal rank; on an equal footing; parallel:
脆弱	cuìruò	(形) of health or feelings) fragile; frail; weak
民间	mínjiān	(形) of the common people; popular; folk
首要	shǒuyào	(形) of the first importance; first; chief:
官方	guānfāng	(形) official:
热泪盈眶	rèlèi yíng kuàng	(形) one's eyes filling with tears

开朗	kāilǎng	(形) open and clear:
开阔	kāikuò	(形) open; wide (square, fields, area)
口头	kǒutóu	(形) oral:
平凡	píngfán	(形) ordinary; common:
陈旧	chénjiù	(形) out-of-date; outmoded; obsolete; old-fashioned
猖狂	chāngkuáng	(形) outrageous (shocking and morally unacceptable); furious (using a lot of effort or strength)
杰出	jiéchū	(形) outstanding; remarkable; prominent:
苍白	cāng bái	(形) pale
娇气	jiāoqì	(形) pampered; spoiled
被动	bèidòng	(形) passive:
合算	hésuàn	(形) paying; worthwhile
安宁	ānníng	(形) peaceful; tranquil (calm and peaceful and without noise, violence, worry, etc.) 2 calm; composed; free from worry
亲身	qīnshēn	(形) personal experience
乌黑	wūhēi	(形) pitch-black; jet-black
一帆风顺	yīfānfēngshùn	(形) plain sailing
充沛	chōngpèi	(形) plentiful; abundant;

贫困	pínkùn	(形) poor:
贫乏	pínfá	(形) poor; short; lacking:
通俗	tōngsú	(形) popular; common:
无能为力	wúnéngwéilì	(形) powerless; impotent:
踏实	tàshí	(形) practical
切实	qièshí	(形) practical; realistic; feasible:
珍稀	zhēnxī	(形) precious and rare
陡峭	dǒuqiào	(形) precipitous (If a slope is precipitous, it is very steep)
精密	jīngmì	(形) precise; accurate:
岂有此理	qǐyǒucǐlǐ	(形) preposterous (very silly or stupid); outrageous:
紧迫	jǐnpò	(形) pressing; urgent; lmmment:
正当	zhèngdàng	(形) proper ; appropriate; legitimate
恰当	qiàdàng	(形) proper; suitable; fitting; appropria te:
昌盛	chāngshèng	(形) prosperous;
兴旺	xīngwàng	(形) prosperous; thriving:
纯洁	chúnjié	(形) pure; unselfish and honest:
敏捷	mǐnjié	(形) quick; nimble; agile:

机智	jīzhì	(形) quick-witted; resourceful
寂静	jìjìng	(形) quiet; still; silent:
急剧	jíjù	(形) rapid; sharp; sudden:
罕见	hǎnjiàn	(形) rare to see; very unusual to see
无赖	wúlài	(形) rascally; scoundrelly; blackguardly (名)

rascal (a dishonest person)

反动	fǎndòng	(形) reactionary (a person who is opposed to

political or social change or new ideas)

现成	xiànchéng	(形) ready-made:
斯文	sīwén	(形) refined; gentle
定期	dìngqí	(形) regular; at regular intervals; periodical:
正规	zhèngguī	(形) regular; standard:
从容不迫	cóngróngbùpò	(形) remain cool-headed and steady
无动于衷	wúdòngyúzhōng	(形) remain indifferent or apathetic
偏僻	piānpì	(形) remote; out-of-the-way:
恭敬	gōngjìng	(形) respectful
雄厚	xiónghòu	(形) rich; solid; abundant (of manpower and

natural resources or wealth)

丰盛	fēngshèng	(形) rich; sumptuous

丰盛	fēngshèng	(形) rich; sumptuous:
波涛汹涌	bōtāoxiōngyǒng	(形) roaring waves
腐朽	fǔxiǔ	(形) rotten; decayed; decadent
粗鲁	cūlǔ	(形) rude; boorish
凹凸	āotú	(形) rugged; (of land) wild and not even
神圣	shénshèng	(形) sacred; holy:
一律	yīlǜ	(形) same; alike; uniform:
圆满	yuánmǎn	(形) satisfactory
知足常乐	zhīzú cháng lè	(形) satisfied with what one has; contentment

(happiness and satisfaction, often because you have everything you need)

| 过瘾 | guòyǐn | (形) satisfy a craving; enjoy oneself to the full; do |

sth. to one's heart's content:

炎热	yánrè	(形) scorching; blazing; burning hot
机密	jīmì	(形) secret; classified; confidential:
资深	zīshēn	(形) Senior; Veteran; Experienced
灵敏	língmǐn	(形) sensitive ; keen; agile; acute:
敏感	mǐngǎn	(形) sensitive; susceptible:
郑重	zhèngzhòng	(形) serious; solemn; earnest:
性感	xìnggǎn	(形) sexy

无耻	wúchǐ	(形) shameless; brazen; impudent:
敏锐	mǐnruì	(形) sharp; acute; keen:
相像	xiāngxiàng	(形) similar; alike
类似	lèisì	(形) similar; analogous:
简陋	jiǎnlòu	(形) simple and crude:
真挚	zhēnzhì	(形) sincere; cordial:
迟缓	chíhuǎn	(形) slow; sluggish:
庄重	zhuāngzhòng	(形) sober (serious and calm); serious (not joking or intended to be funny)
柔和	róuhé	(形) soft; gentle; mild:
庄严	zhuāngyán	(形) solemn; stately; imposing
扎实	zhāshi	(形) solid; sound; down-to-earth:
坚实	jiānshí	(形) solid; substantial:
宽敞	kuānchǎng	(形) spaclous; roomy
美妙	Měimiào	(形) splendid; wonderful; beautiful:
自发	zì fà	(形) spontaneous
滔滔不绝	tāotāo bù jué	(形) spout eloquent speeches
严厉	yánlì	(形) stern; severe:

严峻	yánjùn	(形) stern; severe; rigorous; grim:
吝啬	lìnsè	(形) stingy; miserly; mean:
吃力	chīlì	(形) strenuous; difficult:
固执	gùzhí	(形) stubborn; obstinate
愚蠢	yúchǔn	(形) stupid; foolish; idiotic
适宜	shìyí	(形) suitable; fit; appropriate :
超级	chāojí	(形) super
优越	yōuyuè	(形) superior; advantageous:
供不应求	gōngbùyìngqiú	(形) supply falls short of demand
惊奇	jīngqí	(形) surprised; amazed
惊讶	jīngyà	(形) surprised; amazed; astonished; astounded
优胜劣汰	yōushèngliètài	(形) Survival of the fittest
挺拔	tǐngbá	(形) tall and straight
理所当然	lǐsuǒdāngrán	(形) That is just as it should be. or This is a matter of course.
任重道远	rènzhòngdàoyuǎn	(形) the burden is heavy and the road is long- shoulder heavy responsibilities
得不偿失	débùchángshī	(形) the loss outweighs the gain
立体	lìtǐ	(形) three dimensional; stereoscopic:

兴隆	xīnglóng	(形) thriving; flourishing:
严密	yánmì	(形) tight; close :
胆怯	dǎnqiè	(形) timid; shy
渺小	miǎoxiǎo	(形) tiny; negligible; in significant (of abstract matters)
疲惫	píbèi	(形) tired out; exhausted
疲倦	píjuàn	(形) tired; fa tigued
雪上加霜	xuěshàngjiāshuāng	(形) to add hail to snow (idiom); one disaster on top of another; to make things worse in a bad situation
举世瞩目	jǔshì zhǔmù	(形) to be the focus of world attention
微不足道	wēibùzúdào	(形) too inferior to be worth mentioning
顽强	wánqiáng	(形) tough; indomitable; staunch; tenacious
丑恶	chǒu'è	(形) ugly; hideous; despicable:
畅通	chàngtōng	(形) unblocked; unimpeded; proceed without hindrance
野蛮	yěmán	(形) uncivilized; savage 2 atrocious; brutal
别扭	bièniu	(形) uncomfortable
冷酷	lěngkù	(形) unfeeling; hard- hearted:

空前绝后　　　kōngqiánjuéhòu　　（形）unique; unprecedented and impossibly difficult to recur

反常　　　fǎncháng　　　（形）unusual; abnormal

异常　　　yìcháng　　　（形）unusual; abnormal:

端正　　　duānzhèng　　　（形）upright; regular:

英勇　　　yīngyǒng　　　（形）valiant; brave:

珍贵　　　zhēnguì　　　（形）valuable; precious:

辽阔　　　liáokuò　　　（形）vast; extensive; boundless:

广阔　　　guǎngkuò　　　（形）vast; wide; broad:

垂直　　　chuízhí　　　（形）vertical

竖　　　shù　　　（形）vertical; upright; perpendicular:

短促　　　duǎncù　　　（形）very brief; short:

昂贵　　　ángguì　　　（形）very expensive; costly

万分　　　wànfēn　　　（形）very much; extremely:

猛烈　　　měngliè　　　（形）vigorous; fierce; violent:

剧烈　　　jùliè　　　（形）violent; acute; severe; fierce:

庸俗　　　yōngsú　　　（形）vulgar; philistine (a person who refuses to see the beauty or the value of art or culture); low:

薄弱　　　bóruò　　　（形）weak; frail:

富裕	fùyù	(形) well-to-do; proꞷperous; well off, rich
力所能及	lìsuǒnéngjí	(形) what is in one's power
家喻户晓	jiāyùhùxiǎo	(形) widely known; known to all:
任性	rènxìng	(形) wilful; self-willed
英明	yīngmíng	(形) wise; brilliant:
高明	gāomíng	(形) wise; brilliant: (名)wise or skilful person:
津津有味	jīnjīn yǒu wèi	(形) with relish (the enjoyment you get from doing something); with gusto (great energy, enthusiasm, and enjoyment); with keen pleasure:
书面	shūmiàn	(形) written; in written form; in writing:
贪婪	tānlán	(形)(书) avaricious; greedy; rapacious

4 Pronouns 代词 dàicí

HSK 1 Pronouns 代词 dàicí (20)

我	wǒ	1 (代) I
你	nǐ	(代) 1 you [second person singular]:
他	tā	(代) 1 he
她	tā	(代) she
我们	wǒmen	(代) we
这里	zhèlǐ	here
这儿	zhè'er	here; now; then:
这	zhè	this:
那	nà	1 (代) that

那儿	nà'er	there; that place
那里	nàlǐ	there; that place
哪	nǎ	(代) 1 which; what:
哪儿	nǎ'er	(代) where; wherever:
哪里	Nǎlǐ	(代) where; wherever:
谁	shuí	1 (代) who:
什么	shénme	(代) what
多少	duōshǎo	2 (代) how many; how much:
几	jǐ	1 (数) how many (less than ten)
怎么	Zěnme	1 (代) [interrogative pronoun]
怎么样	zěnme yàng	1 (代) how [used as a predicative or complement]:

HSK 2 Pronouns 代词 dàicí (5)

您	nín	(代) (敬) you (respect way)
它	tā	(代) [neuter gender] it
大家	dàjiā	1 (代) all; everybody

每   měi   1 (代) every; each:

为什么   wèishéme   (代) why; why (or how) is it that

HSK 3 Pronouns 代词 dàicí (2)
其他   qítā   (代) other; else: HSK 3 new

自己   zìjǐ   1 (代) oneself:

HSK 4 Pronouns 代词 dàicí (8)
等   děng   (代) and so on; etc.:

各   gè   (代) each; every:

俩   liǎ   (代) (口) two (of people)

其次   qícì   (代) next; secondly; then:

任何   rènhé   (代) any; whatever:

所有   suǒyǒu   (代) all; what you have

咱们   zánmen   (代) we [including both the speaker and the person or persons spoken to]

另外   lìngwài   (代) in addition; moreover; besides; other; another

HSK 5 Pronouns 代词 dàicí (5)

某	mǒu	(代) certain; some:
彼此	bǐcǐ	(代) each other; one another
各自	gèzì	(代) each; respective:
如何	rúhé	(代) how; what :
其余	qíyú	(代) the rest; the remainder:

HSK 6 Pronouns 代词 dàicí (6)

人家   rénjiā   (代) [used to refer to people other than oneself] other people:

诸位	zhūwèi	(代) (敬) : you
咋	zǎ	(代) (informal, oral) how; why
啥	shà	(代) (informal, oral) what
大伙儿	dàhuǒ er	(代) we all; all of us
若干	ruògān	(代) a certain number:

5 Numeral 数词 shù cí

一   yī   1 (数) one:

二   èr   1 (数) two:

三   sān   1 (数) three:

四   sì   (数) four

五   wǔ   (数) five:

六   liù   (数) six

七   qī   seven

八   bā   eight

九   jiǔ   nine

十   shí   1 (数) ten:

零　　　　　líng　　1 (数) zero sign (0); naught:

HSK 2 Numeral 数词 shù cí (4)

两　　　　　liǎng　　　　1 (数) two:

百　　　　　bǎi　　　　　1 (数) hundred

千　　　　　qiān　　　　　1 (数) thousand:

第一　　　　dì yī　　　　　(形) first; primary; foremost:

HSK 3 Numeral 数词 shù cí (1)

万　　　　　wàn　　　　　1 (数) 1 ten thousand

HSK 4 Numeral 数词 shù cí (2)

… 分之 …　…　fēn zhī…　　　　(数) (of) , like: 1/5, 1 tenth…

亿　　　　　yì　　　　　　(数) a hundred of million

HSK 5 Numeral 数词 shù cí (0)
NO NEW Numeral in HSK 5

You can have a rest, no vocabulary in this category.

HSK 6 Numeral 数词 shù cí (0)
No numeral vocab in HSK 6. Luky!

6 Classifier; Measure Word (MW) 量词 liàngcí

HSK 1 Classifier; Measure Word (MW) 量词 liàngcí (5)

个   gè   1 (量) [the measure word most extensively used esp. before

nouns which do not have special measure words of their own]:

岁   suì   1 (名) year:

本   běn   11 [for books, albums, etc.]

些   xiē   1 (量) some:

块   kuài   1 (名) piece; lump; cube; chunk;

       2 (量) [for a slice or chunk of sth.]

HSK 2 Classifier; Measure Word (MW) 量词 liàngcí (5)

次   cì   (量) time; occurrence

公斤   gōngjīn   (量) (名) kilogram (kg)

元   yuán   (量) dollar

件   jiàn   1 (量) [indicating those things which can be counted] :

张   zhāng   5 (量) for flat things like paper, table, bed etc.

HSK 3 Classifier; Measure Word (MW) 量词 liàngcí (7)

包   bāo   9 (量) [for packages, bundles, etc.] :

一包香烟   yī bāoxiāngyān   a packet (or pack) of cigarettes.

包   bāo   8 (名) bag:

书包	shūbāo	school bag

辆	liàng	(量) (for vehicles):
双	shuāng	4 (量) pair:
种	zhǒng	5 (量) kind; type; sort:
条	tiáo	(量) MW for long things
碗	wǎn	2 (量) a bowl of

一碗牛肉汁	yī wǎn niúròu zhī	a bowl of beef broth

碗	wǎn	1 (名) bowl
饭碗	fànwǎn	(名) 1 rice bowl
饭碗	fànwǎn	2 job; means of livelihood:

位	wèi	(量) [polite form] :

四位客人	sì wèi kèrén	four guests

HSK 4 Classifier; Measure Word (MW) 量词 liàngcí (10)

倍	bèi	(量) times: -fold:
遍	biàn	(量) [indicating the process of an action from beginning to end] time, times

场	chǎng	(量) [said of something which has happened] :
顿	dùn	(量) （used for number of times of scold, meal, persuade ）
朵	duǒ	(量) (for flower, cloud)
份	fèn	(量) (for gift, etc)
棵	kē	(量) (used for trees, plants.)
篇	piān	(量) a piece of writing
趟	tàng	(量) [for trip]
座	zuò	(量) [for large and solid thing]

HSK 5 Classifier; Measure Word (MW) 量词 liàngcí (18)

匹	pǐ	(量) [for horses, etc.]:
片	piàn	(量) [for things in slices]; (名) a flat; thin piece;
幅	fú	(量) [for cloth, painting, etc.] a piece
粒	lì	(量) [for grain-like things] (名) grain; granule; pellet:
届	jiè	(量) [used before a regular meeting or each year's graduates]: session; year's
团	tuán	(量) a ball of; a lump of
批	pī	(量) batch; lot; group:

厘米	límǐ	(量) centimeter
颗	kē	(量) Classifier; Measure Word (MW) for a small and roundish (as a bean, pearl, etc.)
滴	dī	(量) drop (动) drip
堆	duī	(量) heap; pile; crowd (动) pile; stack:
项	xiàng	(量) item:
则	zé	(量) item; paragraph:
升	shēng	(量) litre
秒	miǎo	(量) second (= 1/ 60 of a minute)
吨	dūn	(量) ton
卷	juǎn	(量) volume 2 examination paper:
阵	zhèn	(量) a period of (wind, laugh, cold etc)

栋	dòng	(量) (for building)
筐	kuāng	(量) (名) basket
番	fān	(量) [for actions which take time or effort]:
艘	sōu	(量) [for boats or ships]
幢	zhuàng	(量) [for buildings] :
束	shù	(量) bundle; bunch; sheaf (动) bind; tie
株	zhū	(量) Measure Word (MW) (for plants and trees)
枚	méi	(量) Measure Word (MW) [for small object]
枝	zhī	(量) Measure Word (MW) [for stick like things or for flowers with a branch]:
副	fù	(量) pair; set (形) deputy; assistant; vice-:
串	chuàn	(量) string; cluster: (动) string together

7 Adverb 副词 fùcí

HSK 1 Adverb 副词 fùcí (5)

不	bù	1 [used to form a negative] :
没	méi	not have; be without
很	hěn	(副) very; quite; awfully:
太	tài	3 (副) excessively; too; over:
都	dōu	1 (副) all; both: dōu

HSK 2 Adverb 副词 fùcí (11)

别	bié	(副)7 don't:
非常	fēicháng	2 (副) very; extremely; highly:
也	yě	1 (副) also; too as well:
还	hái	(副) 1 still; yet:

| 最 | zuì | (副) [indicating the superlative degree]: |

| 真 | zhēn | 3 (副) really; truly; indeed: |

| 正在 | zhèngzài | (副) [to indicate an action in progress] in process of; in |

course of:

| 已经 | yǐjīng | (副) already: |

| 一起 | yīqǐ | (副) Together; Together with |

| 再 | zài | 1 (副) again; once more |

| 就 | jiù | 7 (副) at once; right away: |

他马上就来

Tā mǎshàng jiù lái

He will come right away

比较   bǐjiào   3 (副) fairly; comparatively; relatively; quite; rather:

我比较喜欢看电影   wǒ bǐjiào xǐhuān kàn diànyǐng   Relatively speaking, I like films.

比较   bǐjiào   (动) 1 compare; contrast:

多么   duōme   (副) [used in an exclamatory or a compound sentence indicating high degree] how; what; however:

更   gèng   (副) even; more; still more; further:

还是   háishì   1 (副) still; nevertheless; all the same:

尽管下雨，运动会还是照常进行   jǐnguǎn xià yǔ, yùndònghuì háishì zhàocháng jìnxíng The sports meet went on as planned despite the rain.

还是   háishì   2 (副) had better: HSK 3 new

你还是戒烟吧，吸烟对身体不好   nǐ háishì jièyān ba, xīyān duì shēntǐ bù hǎo   You had better quit smoking. It's harmful to your health.

还是   háishì   3 (连) or: HSK 3 new

我今天带雨伞还是雨衣？　　　Wǒ jīntiān dài yǔsǎn háishì yǔyī.　　Should I bring an umbrella or raincoat today?

或者　　　huòzhě　　　1 (副) perhaps; maybe:

快点走，或者还赶得上末班车　　　kuài diǎn zǒu, huòzhě hái gǎndéshàng mòbānchē　Hurry up, and we may catch the last bus.

或者　　　huòzhě　　　2 (连) or; either . . . or. . . :

请把这本书给李老师或者他的女儿。　　　Qǐng bǎ zhè běn shū gěi lǐ lǎoshī huòzhě tā de nǚ'ér. Please give pass this book to teacher Lee or his daughter.

几乎　　　jīhū　　　(副) nearly; almost; practically:

极　　　jí　　　3 (副) extremely; exceedingly:

经常　　　jīngcháng　　2 (副) frequently; constantly; regularly; often:

大家最好经常交换意见　　　dàjiā zuì hǎo jīngcháng jiāohuàn yìjiàn　　We'd better regularly exchange views among ourselves.

他经常帮助他人　　　tā jīngcháng bāngzhù tārén　　He never fails to help others

马上　　　　　măshàng　　　　　(副) at once; straight away; right away; immediately:

其实　　　　　Qí shí　　　　　(副) actually; in fact; as a matter of fact

然后　　　　　ránhòu　　　　　(副) then; after that; afterwards

特别　　　　　tèbié　　　　　2 (副) especially; particularly

时间过得特别快　　　shíjiānguò dé tèbié kuài　　The time sped quickly by.

特别　　　　　tèbié　　　　　1 (形) special; particular; out of the ordinary:

特别风味　　tèbié fēngwèi　　　an unusual flavour

特别的式样　　　tèbié de shìyàng　　special type

突然　　　　　túrán　2 (副) suddenly

突然停止　　túrán tíngzhǐ suddenly stop; stop short

突然　　　　　túrán　1 (形) sudden; abrupt; unexpected:

这件事来得太突然了。Zhè jiàn shì láidé tài túránle.　　This incident came too suddenly.

先　　　　　xiān　　　　(副) 1 earlier; before; first; in advance:

先来先吃　xiān lái xiān chī　First come, first served.

一定　　　　yīdìng　　　4 (副) certainly; surely; necessarily:

他一定会成功　　tā yīdìng huì chénggōng　　He will surely succeed.

一共　　　　yīgòng　　　(副) altogether; in all; all told:

一边　　　　yībiān　　　2 (副) [indicating two simultaneous actions] at the same time; simultaneously:

他一边往前走, 一边拉开嗓子唱着歌儿

tā yībiān wǎng qián zǒu, yībiān lā kāi sǎngzi chàngzhe gē er

He strolled along, singing at the top of his voice.

一边...一边...　　yībiān... yībiān...

[used before two verbs respectively to indicate simultaneous actions]

他一边上网，一边听音乐。

tā yībiān shàngwǎng, yībiān tīng yīnyuè.

He listened to music while surfing the Internet.

一直　　　　yīzhí　　　　1 (副) straight:

一直走　　　yīzhí zǒu　　　go straight on

一直　　　　yīzhí　　　　2 (副) continuously; always; all along; all the way :

雨一直下了一天一夜

yǔ yīzhí xiàle yītiān yīyè

It has been raining the whole day and night

才　　　　cái　　（副）1 [used before a proverb to indicate that sth. has just happened or is rather late by general standards] [(preceded by an expression of time) not until]表示事情发生得晚或结束得晚:

昨晚十二点才睡。　　Zuó wǎn shí'èr diǎn cái shuì.　　slept (as late as) twelve o'clock last night.

他四十岁才结婚　　tā sìshí suì cái jiéhūn　　He got married (as late as) when he was forty

你怎么才来?　　nǐ zěnme cái lái?　Why are you so late?

又　　　　yòu　　　2 (副) [indicating the simultaneous existence of several conditions or characteristics]:

又高又大　　　　yòu gāo yòu dà　　tall and big.

越…越…　　　　yuè…yuè…　　　(副) the more... the more. …

越多越好　yuè duō yuè hǎo　the more the better

雨越下越大。　　Yǔ yuè xiàyuè dà. The rain is getting bigger.

越来越…　　Yuè lái yuè...　　more and more ...

她越来越漂亮。　Tā yuè lái yuè piàoliang. She was more beautiful.

他长得越来越高。　　Tā zhǎng dé yuè lái yuè gāo.　　He grows more and more taller.

这孩子吃得越来越多　　Zhè háizi chī dé yuè lái yuè duō This child eat more and more

只　　　　zhǐ　　　　(副) only; merely:

屋里只有我一个人　　wū li zhǐyǒu wǒ yīgèrén　　　I was alone in the room.

终于　　　zhōngyú　　　(副) at last; in the end

他终于试验成功。　　Tā zhōngyú shìyàn chénggōng.　Finally he succeeded in

his experiment

她终于平静下来了　　tā zhōngyú píngjìng xiàláile　　She calmed down at last.

HSK 4 Adverb 副词 fùcí (38)

故意	gùyì	(副) purposely; intentionally; deliberately:
按时	ànshí	(副) on time; on schedule:
本来	běnlái	(副) originally
不得不	bùdé bù	(副)have no choice (or option) but to; cannot but; have to:
重新	chóngxīn	(副) again; anew; afresh: -
从来	cónglái	(副) always; all along:
大概	dàgài	(副) probably:
到底	dàodǐ	(副) at last; finally; in the end
大约	dàyuē	(副) approximately; about:
刚刚	Gānggāng	(副) just; only; exactly
果然	guǒrán	(副) really; as expected; sure enough:
忽然	Hūrán	(副) suddenly; all of a sudden
互相	hùxiāng	(副) mutual; mutually:

竟然	jìngrán	(副) unexpectedly; to one's surprise; actually:
极其	jíqí	(副) most; extremely; exceedingly:
究竟	Jiùjìng	(副) [used in an interrogative sentence to make further inquiries] actually; exactly:
恐怕	kǒngpà	(副) I'm afraid:
难道	nándào	(副) [make an emphatic rhetorical question]:
偶尔	ǒu'ěr	(副) once in a long while; occasionally:
千万	qiān wàn	(副) [used of exhortation or a friendly warning]: must
却	què	(副) but; yet; however:
确实	quèshí	(副) really; indeed 2 (形) true; certain; reliable:
仍然	réngrán	(副) still; yet
稍微	shāowéi	(副) a little; slightly:
甚至	shènzhì	(副) even; (go) so far as to; so much so that:
十分	shífēn	(副) very; fully; utterly; extremely:
首先	shǒuxiān	(副) first; first of all
顺便	shùnbiàn	(副) by the way; incidentally; in passing:
挺	tǐng	(副) very; rather; quite :
往往	wǎngwǎng	(副) often; frequently; more often than not

完全　　　　wánquán　　　(副) completely; fully; wholly; entirely; absolutely: (形)
complete; whole:

也许　　　　yěxǔ　　　　(副) perhaps; probably; maybe:

永远　　　　yǒngyuǎn　　(副) always ; forever; ever

尤其　　　　yóuqí　　　　(副) especially; particularly:

只好　　　　Zhǐhǎo　　　(副) have to:

至少　　　　zhìshǎo　　　(副) at (the) least :

逐渐　　　　zhújiàn　　　(副) gradually:

HSK 5 Adverb 副词 fùcí (40)

毕竟　　　　bìjìng　　　　(副) after all; all in all; in the final analysis

总共　　　　zǒnggòng　　(副) all together; in all:

单独　　　　dāndú　　　　(副) alone; by oneself; on one's own:

反正　　　　fǎnzhèng　　(副) anyway; anyhow; in any case:

格外　　　　géwài　　　　(副) especially; exceptionally:

凡是　　　　fánshì　　　　(副) every; any; all:

总算　　　　zǒngsuàn　　(副) finally; at last:

特意	tèyì	(副) for a special purpose; specially
幸亏	xìngkuī	(副) fortunately; luckily
始终	shǐzhōng	(副) from start to finish; all along; through out:
赶快	gǎnkuài	(副) hasten; at once; quickly:
立即	lìjí	(副) immediately; at once:
立刻	lìkè	(副) immediately; at once; right away:
的确	díquè	(副) indeed; really:
反而	fǎn'ér	(副) instead; on the contrary:
似乎	sìhū	(副) it seems; as if:
赶紧	gǎnjǐn	(副) lose no time; hasten
未必	wèibì	(副) may not; not necessarily :
更加	gèngjiā	(副) more; still more; even more:
不必	bùbì	(副) need not; not have to:
怪不得	guàibùdé	(副) no wonder; so that's why:
不见得	bùjiàn dé	(副) not necessarily; not likely:
曾经	céngjīng	(副) once; formerly :
陆续	lùxù	(副) one after another; in succession:
再三	zài sān	(副) over and over

说不定	shuō bu dìng	(副) perhaps; maybe:
亲自	qīnzì	(副) personally; in person:
连忙	liánmáng	(副) promptly; at once:
悄悄	qiāoqiāo	(副) quietly; stealthily:
反复	fǎnfù	(副) repeatedly; again and again; over and over again
简直	jiǎnzhí	(副) simply; at all:
依然	yīrán	(副) still; as before:
轮流	lúnliú	(副) take turns; do sth. in turn:
何必	Hébì	(副) there is no need; why:
至今	zhìjīn	(副) to date; until now; up to now.
尽量	jǐnliàng	(副) to the best of one's ability; as far as possible:
不免	bùmiǎn	(副) unavoidable
不断	bùduàn	(副) unceasing; uninterrupted; continuous; constant:
居然	jūrán	(副) unexpectedly; to one's surprise:
是否	shìfǒu	(副) whether or not; whether; if:

HSK 6 Adverb 副词 fùcí (83)

皆   jiē   (副) (书) all; each and every:

归根到底   guīgēn dàodǐ   (副) (also 归根结底) in the final analysis; Ultimately ; come to the end

就近   jiùjìn   (副) (do or get sth.) at a nearby place; in the neighbourhood; without having to go far.

亦   yì   (副) (书) also; too:

勿   wù   (副) [indicating prohibition] no

固然   gùrán   (副) [used to acknowledge a fact in order to make a contrary statement which is the speaker's real purpose] no doubt; it is true:

照样   zhàoyàng   (副) 1 after a pattern or model 2 in the same old way; as before

终究   zhōngjiù   (副) after all; in the end

成天   chéngtiān   (副) All day; all the time

统统   tǒngtǒng   (副) all; completely; entirely; lock, stock and barrel:

向来   xiànglái   (副) always; all along:

依旧	yījiù	(副) as before; still:
仍旧	réngjiù	(副) as before; still; yet:
尽快	jǐnkuài	(副) as quickly (or soon, early) as possible:
及早	jízǎo	(副) at an early date; as soon as possible; before it is too late:
随意	suíyì	(副) at will; as one pleases
大不了	dàbùliǎo	(副) at worst; if worst comes to worst
即将	jíjiāng	(副) be about to; be on the point of:
恰巧	qiàqiǎo	(副) by chance; fortunately: Happened
不由得	bùyóudé	(副) cannot help; cannot but
不禁	bùjīn	(副) can't help (doing sth.) ; can't refrain from:
势必	shìbì	(副) certainly will ; be bound to:
必定	bìdìng	(副) certainly; surely:
一向	yīxiàng	(副) consistently; all along
随手	suíshǒu	(副) conveniently (when doing sth.); without extra trouble:
偏偏	piānpiān	(副) deliberately:
并非	bìngfēi	(副) Does not
足以	zúyǐ	(副) enough; sufficient :

暂且	zànqiě	(副) for the time being; for the moment:
幸好	xìnghǎo	(副) fortunately; luckily
不时	bùshí	(副) from time to time
时而	shí'ér	(副) from time to time; sometimes 2 now... now...;

sometimes. . .sometimes...

大致	dàzhì	(副) generally; roughly; approximately; more or less
全力以赴	quánlì yǐ fù	(副) go all out; spare no effort
无从	wúcóng	(副) have no way (of doing sth.); not be in a

position (to do sth.) :

迎面	Yíngmiàn	(副) head-on; in one's face:
顿时	dùnshí	(副) immediately; at once
随即	suíjí	(副) immediately; presently
预先	yùxiān	(副) in advance; beforehand:
本着	běnzhe	(副) in line with; in the light of; in conformity with
日益	rìyì	(副) increasingly; day by day:
断断续续	duànduàn xù xù	(副) intermittently:
一如既往	yīrújìwǎng	(副) just as in the past; as before; as always:
恰到好处	qiàdàohǎochù	(副) Just perfect; Just the right
精心	jīngxīn	(副) meticulously; painstakingly; elaborately:

务必	wùbì	(副) must; be sure to:
毫无	háo wú	(副) none; no at all
无非	wúfēi	(副) nothing but; no more than; simply; only:
明明	míngmíng	(副) obviously; undoubtedly:
时常	shícháng	(副) often; frequently
接连	jiēlián	(副) on end; in a row; in succession:
成心	chéng xīn	(副) on purpose; intentionally; deliberately:
反倒	fǎndào	(副) on the contrary
当场	dāngchǎng	(副) on the spot; then and there:
大体	dàtǐ	(副) on the whole; by and large; roughly:
一度	yī dù	(副) once; on one occasion; for a time:
依次	yīcì	(副) one by one in due order.
唯独	wéi dú	(副) only, exception; alone
公然	gōngrán	(副) openly; brazenly
或许	huòxǔ	(副) perhaps; maybe:
私自	sīzì	(副) privately; secretly; without permission:
默默	mòmò	(副) quietly; silently:
颇	pō	(副) quite; rather; considerably:

未免	wèimiǎn	(副) rather; a bit too truly:
斩钉截铁	zhǎndīngjiétiě	(副) resolute and decisive
毅然	yìrán	(副) resolutely; firmly; determinedly
略微	lüèwēi	(副) slightly; a little; somewhat:
竭尽全力	jiéjìn quánlì	(副) spare no effort; do one's utmost; do all one can
专程	zhuānchéng	(副) special trip
姑且	gūqiě	(副) tentatively; for the time being:
不妨	bùfáng	(副) there is no harm in; might as well:
一再	yīzài	(副) time and again; again and again; repeatedly:
屡次	lǚcì	(副) time and again; repeatedly:
当面	dāngmiàn	(副) to sb. 's face; in sb. 's presence:
迫不及待	pòbùjídài	(副) too impatient to wait
过于	guòyú	(副) too unduly; excessively:

不料　　　bùliào　　　(副) unexpectedly; to one's surprise

任意　　　rènyì　　　(副) wantonly; wilfully:

理直气壮　lǐzhíqìzhuàng　(副) with perfect assurance

擅自　　　shànzì　　　(副) without authorization:

索性　　　suǒxìng　　　(副) without hesitation; simply; might as well; why not

大肆　　　dàsì　　　(副) without restraint; wantonly:

逐年　　　zhúnián　　　(副) year by year; year after year; with each passing year

8 Conjunction 连词 liáncí

HSK 1 Conjunction 连词 liáncí (1)
和   hé   7 (连) and : hé

HSK 2 Conjunction 连词 liáncí (3)
因为   yīnwèi   (连) because; for; on account of

所以   suǒyǐ   1 (连) [used to indicate cause and effect] so; therefore; as

a result:

但是   dànshì   (连) but; yet; still; nevertheless

HSK 3 Conjunction 连词 liáncí (5)
而且   érqiě   (连) and also; moreover; in addition:

他不但迟到了，还忘了带书。

Tā bùdàn chídàole, hái wàngle dài shū.

Not only did he turn up late, he also forgot his books.

他不但很懂画，而且自己画得也不错

tā bùdàn hěn dǒng huà, érqiě zìjǐ huà de yě bùcuò

He knows a lot about painting, and he paints well himself.

不仅下了雪，而且下得很大

bùjǐn xiàle xuě, érqiě xià de hěn dà

It not only snowed but also snowed heavily

跟　　gēn　(连) and also (同 和，表示联合关系）

车上装的是机器跟材料。　　Chē shàngzhuāng de shì jīqì gēn cáiliào.

The car is loaded with machinery and materials.

他的胳膊跟大腿都受了伤。　Tā de gēbó gēn dàtuǐ dōu shòule shāng.

His arm and thigh were injured.

跟　　　　gēn　　3 (介) [denoting the same function as that of 和，同] with :

我跟他一样高　　wǒ gēn tā yīyàng gāo　　He and I are of the same height.

我跟你一起去　　wǒ gēn nǐ yīqǐ qù　　　I'll go with you.

如果　　　rúguǒ　　　(连) if; in case; in the event of:

虽然　　　suīrán　　　(连) though; although

或者 huòzhě   2 (连) or; either . . . or. . . :

请把这本书给李老师或者他的女儿。

Qǐng bǎ zhè běn shū gěi lǐ lǎoshī huòzhě tā de nǚ'ér.

Please give pass this book to teacher Lee or his daughter.

或者 huòzhě   1 (副) perhaps; maybe:

快点走，或者还赶得上末班车

kuài diǎn zǒu, huòzhě hái gǎndéshàng mòbānchē

Hurry up, and we may catch the last bus.

HSK 4 Conjunction 连词 liáncí (15)

并且	bìngqiě	(连) and; besides; moreover; furthermore
不但	bùdàn	(连) not only:
不过	bùguò	(连) only; merely; no more than:
不仅	bùjǐn	(连) not the only one:

而	ér	(连) express coordination
否则	fŏuzé	(连) otherwise; if not; or else:
尽管	jǐnguǎn	(连) though; even though; in spite of; despite
既然	jìrán	(连) since; as; now that:
即使	jíshǐ	(连) even; even if; even though:
可是	kěshì	(连) but; yet; however:
然而	rán'ér	(连) yet; but; however
无论	wúlùn	(连) no matter what, how, etc.; regardless of:
因此	yīncǐ	(连) therefore; for this reason; consequently
于是	yú shì	(连) thereupon; hence; consequently; as a result
只要	zhǐyào	(连) so long as; provided:

HSK 5 Conjunction 连词 liáncí (19)

除非 chúfēi (连) [often used in conjunction with 才，否则，不然，etc. to indicate that what follows is a necessary condition]: only if; unless:

与其 yǔqí (连) [used in the context of making a decision after weighing the pros and cons]:

至于	zhìyú	(连) as for; as to:
以及	yǐjí	(连) as well as; along with; and
此外	cǐwài	(连) besides; moreover; in addltlon
哪怕	Nǎpà	(连) even; even if; even though; no matter how:
从此	cóngcǐ	(连) from now on; since then; henceforth; from this time on
要是	yàoshi	(连) if, suppose, in case
假如	jiǎrú	(连) if; supposing; in case:
总之	zǒngzhī	(连) in a word; in short
可见	kějiàn	(连) it is thus clear (or evident, obvious) that:
万一	wàn yī	(连) just in case; if by any chance 2 (名) contingency; eventuality
何况	Hékuàng	(连) much less; let alone:
难怪	nánguài	(连) no wonder:
不然	bùrán	(连) or else; otherwise; if not: (形) not so
要不	yào bù	(连) otherwise; or else; or:
因而	yīn'ér	(连) thus; as a result; with the result that
从而	cóng'ér	(连) thus; thereby
宁可	nìngkě	(连) would rather; better:

以至   yǐzhì   (连) [indicating an unpleasant result] with the result that; consequently:

以致   yǐzhì   (连) [indicating an unpleasant result] with the result that; consequently:

即便   jíbiàn   (连) even if

假使   jiǎshǐ   (连) if; in case; in the event that:

倘若   tǎngruò   (连) if; supposing; in case

总而言之   zǒng'éryánzhī   (连) in a word; in short

以免   yǐmiǎn   (连) in order to avoid or prevent:

况且   kuàngqiě   (连) moreover; besides

反之   fǎnzhī   (连) otherwise; conversely; on the contrary

要不然   yào bùrán   (连) otherwise; or else; or:

进而	jìn'ér	(连) proceed to the next step; and then
免得	miǎndé	(连) so as not to; so as to avoid:
以便	yǐbiàn	(连) so that; in order to; so as to; with the aim of; for the purpose of:
迄今为止	qìjīn wéizhǐ	(连) up to now; so far
宁愿	nìngyuàn	(连) would ra ther; better:
宁肯	nìngkěn	(连) would rather; better

9 Preposition 介词 jiècí

HSK 1 Preposition 介词 jiècí (1)
在   zài   2 [indicating the position of a person or thing]:

HSK 2 Preposition 介词 jiècí (5)
从   cóng   1 (介) [used to indicate the starting point] from; pass by:

对   duì   11 (介): to; towards

比   bǐ   (介) 5 [indicating difference in manner or degree by

comparison] :

向   xiàng   4 (介) to; towards:

离   lí   (介) 2 off; away; from; (away from, distance from)

HSK 3 Preposition 介词 jiècí (6)
关于   guānyú   (介) aboul; on; with regard to; concerning:

一本关于中国的书   yī běn guānyú zhōngguó de shū

a book about China.

把   bǎ   [The usage of 把 often causes inversion with the object placed before the verb] Have sth Done;

请把门关上   qǐng bǎmén guānshàng   Shut the door, please.

把书合上   bǎ shū hé shàng   close the book

被   bèi   3 used before a notional verb to indicate that the subject is the receiver]:

他被蛇咬伤了   tā bèi shé yǎo shāngle   He was bitten by a snake.

为   wèi   5 (介) [used together with 所 to indicate a passive structure] :

为情所困   wéiqíngsuǒkùn   Troubled by love; Lovesick

为了   wèi le   In order to, for (the purpose of)

为了玩游戏，他连饭都忘了。

Wèile wán yóuxì, tā lián fàn dōu wàngle.

In order to play the game, he even have forgotten to eat.

为了让自己更健康，他每天都花一个小时去锻炼身体。

Wèile ràng zìjǐ gèng jiànkāng, tā měitiān dū huā yīgè xiǎoshí qù duànliàn shēntǐ.

In order to make himselfe more healthy, he spent an hour a day to exercise.

为一些小事吵嘴

wéi yīxiē xiǎoshì chǎozuǐ

bickering over small matters

除了   chúle   (介) except:

除了她，谁也不会唱这支歌

chúle tā, shuí yě bù huì chàng zhè zhī gē

No one can sing this song except her

除了星期一和星期三，我每天都有工作。

Chúle xīngqí yī hè xīngqísān, wǒ měitiān dū yǒu gōngzuò

Except for Mondays and Wednesdays, I have work every day.

HSK 4 Preposition 介词 jiècí (8)

当	dāng	(介) just at (a certain time or place)
连	lián	(介) even:
随着	suízhe	(介) along with; in the wake of:
往	wǎng	(介) in the direction of; to; toward:
以	yǐ	(介) according to: - 级别
由	yóu	(介) because of; due to
由于	yóuyú	(介) due to; owing to; thanks to; as a result of
与	yǔ	(介) with; to:

HSK 5 Preposition 介词 jiècí (2)

对于	duìyú	(介) regarding; as far as
自从	zìcóng	(介) since; from

| 鉴于 | jiànyú | (介) in view of; seeing that: |
| 连同 | liántóng | (介) together with; including |

10 Particle 助词 zhùcí

HSK 1 Particle 助词 zhùcí (4)

的   de   4 [used after a pronoun] : show possession   de

了   le   to express a completed action

吗   ma   (助) [used at the end of a declarative sentence to transform it

into a question]:

呢   ne   (助) 1 [used at the end of an interrogative sentence]:

HSK 2 Particle 助词 zhùcí (4)

得   de   1 (助)[used between a verb or an adjective and its

complement to indicate result, possibility or degree]

着   zhe   1 (助) [indicating an action in progress] :

过   guò   1 (助) [expressing the completion of action]

吧   Ba   1 (助) [used at the end of a sentence to indicate

suggestion, requestor command]

HSK 3 Particle 助词 zhùcí (2)

地   de   (助) [used after an adjective, a noun or a phrase to form an adverbial adjunct before the verb] :

Adjective + 地 + Verb: Change Adjective to adverb

天渐渐地冷了   Tiān jiànjiàn de lěngle   It was getting cold

果树渐渐地绿了。   guǒshù jiànjiàn de lùle.   The fruit trees are gradually green.

天渐渐地黑了。   Tiān jiànjiàn de hēile.   It was getting dark.

Noun + 地 + Verb: Change Noun to adverb

系统性地总结了经验。 Xìtǒng xìng dì zǒngjiéle jīngyàn.   Systematically summarizes the experience.

科学地总结了经验。   Kēxué de zǒngjiéle jīngyàn.   Scientifically sum up the experience.

A phrase + 地 + Verb: Change Phrase to adverb

孩子一天一天地长大了。　　　　Háizi yītiān yī tiāndì zhǎng dàle.　　　　Children grow up day by day.

A Verb phrase + 地 + Verb: Change Verb Phrase to adverb

合理地安排和使用时间

Hélǐ de ānpái hé shǐyòng shíjiān

Reasonably to arrange and use of time

忘我地工作　　　　wàngwǒ dì gōngzuò　　　　work selflessly

实事求是地处理问题。　shíshìqiúshì de chǔlǐ wèntí.　　　　a realistic approach to the problem.

HSK 4 Particle 助词 zhùcí (0)
You can have a rest, no vocabulary in this category.

HSK 5 Particle 助词 zhùcí (1)
似的　　　　shì de　　　　(助) [indicating similarity] :

嘛   ma   (助) [used within a sentence to mark a pause] :

啦   la   (助) [the representation of the combined sounds " le" and "a" , denoting exclamation, interrogation, etc.] :

左右   zuǒyòu   (助) about; more or less (名) the left and right sides (动) control; influence

而已   éryǐ   (助) that is all; nothing more:

11 Interjection[14] 叹词 tàn cí

HSK 1 叹词 Interjection tàn cí (1)

喂　　　　wèi　　1 (叹) [used in greeting or to attract attention] hello; hey:

HSK 2 叹词 Interjection tàn cí (0)

You can have a rest, no vocabulary in this category.

HSK 3 叹词 Interjection tàn cí (0)

You can have a rest, no vocabulary in this category.

HSK 4 叹词 Interjection tàn cí (1)

呀　　　　ya　　　　(叹) [indicating surprise] ah; oh:

HSK 5 叹词 Interjection tàn cí (1)

唉　　　　āi　　　　(叹)（a sigh of sadness or regret）

HSK 6 叹词 Interjection tàn cí (5)

哼　　　　hēng　　　(叹) [expressing dissatisfaction or doubt] humph

---

[14]感叹词 a word that is used to show a short sudden expression of emotion

"Hey!" is an interjection.　　hey 是个感叹词。

哦	Ó	(叹) [indicating doubt]:
嗯	ń	(叹) [used for having words repeated when not heard]:
嘿	hēi	(叹) hey:
唉哟	āi yō	(叹) Ouch! ; Hey!

12 Onomatopoeia[15] 象声词 xiàngshēngcí

HSK 1 象声词 xiàngshēngcí Onomatopoeia (0)
You can have a rest, no vocabulary in this category.

HSK 2 象声词 xiàngshēngcí Onomatopoeia (0)
You can have a rest, no vocabulary in this category.

HSK 3 象声词 xiàngshēngcí Onomatopoeia (0)
You can have a rest, no vocabulary in this category.

---

[15] 拟声法；拟声词，象声词 the act of creating or using words that include sounds that are similar to the noises the words refer to

HSK 4 象声词 xiàngshēngcí Onomatopoeia (0)
You can have a rest, no vocabulary in this category.

HSK 5 象声词 xiàngshēngcí Onomatopoeia (0)
You can have a rest, no vocabulary in this category.

HSK 6 象声词 xiàngshēngcí Onomatopoeia (2)

哇   wa   (象) [sound of vomiting and crying]

嗨   hāi   (象) hi, hey

哇，我学完六级了！ Cheers!

Challenge yourself to take one more step forward to your Proficiency and Success：

HSK 9000 Chinese Vocabulary Version 2020 - HSK 9000 Chinese Vocabulary

for your Proficiency and Success V2021-The comprehensive Vocabulary with the

best possible English translation for HSK, IB Chinese A & B, GCE A1, A2, SAT,

AP Chinese.   http://edeo.biz/6067

This is the vocabulary list for New HSK 9! Is there any HSK 9? Yes, the initial

Classification from 1992 to 2009. There are total 8000 vocabularies. New HSK

(after 2009) which cut the vocabulary to 5000, just want to set a lower passing bar

for students who take Chinese as second language or foreign language.

There are around 100,000 vocabularies in comprehensive Chinese dictionary. The

new HSK 5000 vocabularies only account for 5%, which is far from enough for

students to continue their college in China taught in Chinese. For advance level

oversea Chinese examinations like IB Chinese_A_Language_and_literature_HL,

IB Chinese_A_Literature_HL, IB Chinese_B_HL, SAT Chinese, AP Chinese,

Edexcel A LEVEL Chinese 9CN0-01,02,03 (OLD 6CN0), Edexcel AS Chinese

8CN0-01,02,03 (OLD 6CN0), CIE IGCSE First Language (0509), CIE IGCSE

Second Language (0523), the vocabulary involved are far more than HSK 5000

vocabularies.

Due to this, we continue to update our HSK 9 Vocabularies with the possible Best

English Translation for your better understanding with our many years' experience

in HSK and GCSE teaching since 2009! By referring oversea Chinese

examinations and China Education Ministry official vocabulary list up to high school, similar to K12 in USA, we choose the full vocabulary list specified by Education Ministry of P.R. China as an addition to our HSK 6 Vocabularies.

The full list summary and comparing with HSK (New after 2009).

甲级词(1033); (HSK 1-4)

乙级词(2018); (HSK 5-6)

丙级词(2202) ; (HSK 6)

丁级词(3569) (HSK 9 before 2009)

We add related vocabularies and more expansions. The total vocabularies are more than 9000.

We also add more sentences to illustrate how to apply certain vocabularies in context. All sentences are chosen from authority resources such as Oxford dictionary, Cambridge dictionary etc.

Many students call it "LIFE SAVING" for their exam. The book give a quick revision for your coming exam! Grab it! Thanks for your support for us creating better contents for you!